OPEN HOUSE

OPEN HOUSE

Conversations with Writers about Community

Edited by Kristina Marie Darling

Tupelo Press

North Adams, Massachusetts

Open House: Conversations with Writers about Community

Edited by Kristina Marie Darling
Library of Congress Cataloging-in-Publication data available upon request.

ISBN-13: 978-1-961209-37-4 (paperback)
ISBN-13: 978-1-961209-48-0 (ebook)

Cover and text design by Allison O'Keefe
Cover art: Sally Spens, *Edge of a Sunlit Morning*

First paperback edition November 2025

Tupelo Press
P.O. Box 1767
North Adams, Massachusetts 01247
(413) 664-9611 / Fax: (413) 664-9711
editor@tupelopress.org / www.tupelopress.org

Tupelo Press is an award-winning independent literary press that publishes fine fiction, non- fiction, and poetry in books that are a joy to hold as well as read. Tupelo Press is a registered 501(c)(3) nonprofit organization, and we rely on public support to carry out our mission of publishing extraordinary work that may be outside the realm of the large commercial publishers. Financial donations are welcome and are tax deductible.

CONTENTS

AN INTRODUCTION: LITERARY ARTS AND THE OPEN DOOR

Kristina Marie Darling

This book is intended to offer a practical guide to building community, fostering collaboration, and inspiring generosity through the creative arts. These original essays feature an accomplished roster of contributors with backgrounds in such diverse fields as literary translation, magazine editing, publishing, higher education, and curriculum design. By featuring successful writers who represent such a wide range of skillsets and career paths, the book is meant to help students envision themselves as leaders in the university and well beyond its boundaries. In a cultural moment where graduates often seek meaningful careers outside of academia, this collection also offers an introduction to alt-ac career paths and the unique opportunities for effecting social change in these roles. Focusing on techniques that have broad applications for high school teachers, nonprofit leaders, community outreach organizations, and college classrooms, each chapter includes an original essay from a contemporary writer, editor, or nonprofit leader in the arts and culminates in a set of original exercises for individuals and groups that focus on empathy, citizenship, and community stewardship. It's an honor to present this volume within the context of Tupelo Press and *Tupelo Quarterly*'s legacy of fostering generosity and understanding through the literary arts. Enjoy!

PART ONE

Collaboration as Community Stewardship: In the Classroom and Beyond

COLLABORATION IS COMMUNITY, OR, "FROM WORK TO TEXT" REVISITED

John James

In a 1984 volume titled *Le bruissement de la langue* (which Richard Howard not inaccurately translates as *The Rustle of Language*, but which of course has other meanings: the "swish," for instance, of the "tongue") Roland Barthes forges a distinction between "work" and "text": the work is "seen," and the text is "demonstrated." The work is "the object of a science of the letter" (i.e., philology), while the text is defined by "a notion of *play*." The work is "held in the hand," and the text is "held in language," etc. (57). Barthes continues at some length, but the thrust of his argument is that works are concrete objects, experienced in books, on broadsides, in the blue glow of the phone. Their status is reaffirmed by their production and reproduction, as well as by their inclusion in syllabi or their appearance in department course listings. The text on the other hand is an imaginative experience. It is generated in the interaction between the reader and the work, and in that sense, its making defies all notions of singular authorship. Simply put, there is no text without a reader. The reader is as much the author of the text as the author her-, him-, or theirself. To read a text is, necessarily, to collaborate.

"Collaboration" stems from the Latin *co-*, which indicates connection or collectivity, and the verb *laborare*, to "labor" or to "work." As I use it in this essay, the term indicates a process of "working-with" that involves more than a single self, mind, or sense of agency. To "collaborate" means to labor together, though this labor can take various forms, many of which I aim to explore in some detail. But if texts are collaborative, so too are works—in all or almost all instances, though often in different ways or to varying degrees. How, then, does the collaborative nature of a "work" complicate the already collaborative act of reading? Does this textual process of "working-with" fundamentally change when we encounter collaborative works? Might these somewhat theoretical forms of collaboration reflect upon our participation in a community or in collaborative productions?

When I say that works are collaborative, I mean that in many senses, more than I can touch on in this rather brief essay. Some of these senses are material in nature, inasmuch as artworks, even written works, manifest in some physical form, whose production is always already an assemblage of many hands. A book must be printed, but by whom? Before that, the language must be typeset, the paper printed, trees felled, products shipped from one location to another. Who performs these activities? Probably the "author"—inasmuch as we can deploy that term without irony—scribbled the poem or story into a notebook or typed it up on a computer. All of those materials have an origin. In short, material processes bear upon the production of works, and therefore bear upon our experience of them. As Marx suggests, all commodities maintain a "physical form" and a "value form" (33), and while the latter term becomes somewhat complicated, it remains inseparable from the physical manifestation of the commodity, as it does from the social and aesthetic "use" of an artwork. Even as mere physical objects, artworks necessitate collaboration.

Beyond these material elements, many distinct *types* of works require a heightened degree of collaboration. Such works include collaborative writing in the more colloquial sense, i.e., as a singular work of multiple makers, but they might also encompass poetic forms that draw on source texts, such as the Italian cento, or experimental modes of linguistic collage. (Timothy Donnelly's "Dream of a Poetry of Defence," for instance, intersperses language from Percy Shelley's "A Defence of Poetry" with that from the 9/11 Commission Report.) It might also index call-and-response forms, such as the Japanese renga, or ekphrastic works, which are necessarily intertextual. It might also include translation. Each of these examples manifests a unique collaborative relationship, which shapes work and text alike. These relationships influence the aesthetic creation of works, as well as our textual experience of them, both of which I explore here.

* * *

Properly speaking, collaborative works are rare in contemporary poetry, and yet rarer are collaborative books. This is in part due to the Romantic myth of the lyric subject: the idea that poems represent the ideas or, most especially, the emotions of a solitary speaker. To one degree or another, this dynamic has deeply influenced poetic production over the last two centuries, especially in the anglophone world. While this model of poetic speakership well predates the *Lyrical Ballads*, the most influential statement to this effect derives from William Wordsworth's preface to that volume. Many poets have taken quite seriously Wordsworth's definition of poetry as the "spontaneous overflow of powerful feelings" (291), while overlooking a crucial qualification to that claim: that poetic meter "has shown to heighten and improve the pleasure which co-exists with it" (304). As it turns out, Wordsworth argues that the structure of poetic form restrains and refines emotion, and he advocates for such refinement as a means of channeling—and ultimately, of mediating—emotional "overflow." Indeed, Wordsworth imagines the poet's labor akin to the "situation of the translator," inasmuch as the poet carries emotion across the mediating boundary of verse structure and locates it, more securely, in the heart and mind of the reader. In so doing, this poet-translator labors with another author, the reader, to generate a new—and newly collaborative—work, filled with meaning and emotion. The idea that Wordsworth, or any major poet from that period, advocates for a singular lyric speaker is in itself a fiction, and ignores the fact that the *Lyrical Ballads* was from the outset a collaborative production.

In poetic practice, however, the myth of the lyric subject has shaped the very grammar of our poems. Wordsworth himself pioneered a form of autobiographical verse, which closely revolves around a first-person lyric speaker, who frequently deploys the first-person pronoun, "I." This appears in stark contrast to only slightly earlier poetry, including what used to be described as "pre-Romantic" verse, much of which is more didactic than anything Wordsworth composed. James Thomson's eighteenth-century georgic poem *The Seasons* contains many "eyes," for instance—a "microscopic eye," a "universal eye," a "philosophic eye"—all of which refigure our perspective, but none of which represent the subjectivity of the poet. The convention of the first-person speaker marks a fundamental shift in the perspective and the modality of anglophone poetry, and for this reason, it remains Wordsworth's most widespread and enduring aesthetic contribution. Today, the vast majority of poems published in the United States heavily deploy the first-person pronoun. Exceptions to this rule are generally considered "experimental" (another term used by Wordsworth) and often justify the absence of that "I" through statements on poetic practice. While such poems have become more frequent since the 1980s, not least with the emergence of Language poetry, such aesthetics continue to hover closer to the margin rather than to the center of American poetry.

The result of this aesthetic inheritance is a poetic ecosystem that subsists, in aesthetic and material ways, on the notion of subjective speakership. It affects the tone and texture of our poems, and fundamentally alters how readers relate to such pieces. This altered relationship is reflected in the literary marketplace, where poetry publishing has become increasingly reliant upon the notion of poetic personae, themselves undoubtedly an offshoot of the lyric speaker. Of course, poems communicate as much through form as through the explicit statements of their speakers. Their ostensible subject matter is often complicated by the mode through which that matter is delivered. As I often tell my students, do not ask what a poem is about. Ask what it *does*. But how does one market a convention, a style, or a technique? An effect? The demand for a poem or a group of poems to speak upon or on behalf of a particular subject, and most especially upon a political subject, often drives the rather circumscribed economy on which poetry publishing relies. That the speaker of such poems embodies an identifiable form—that they appear, essentially, as a character—is crucial to this model.

This is not necessarily a bad thing. Recent trends have utilized this market effect to elevate voices of color, transgender voices, and the voices of disabled people, and the world is most definitely better for it. In terms of collaborative work, however, it imposes certain limitations. If the idea of singular lyric speakership limits the production of collaborative works, it also curbs opportunities for publication. This does not mean that such works have not appeared, especially over the last half-century, but even here their collaborative nature has too frequently escaped notice. When John Ashbery and James Schuyler's hilarious collaborative novel *A Nest of Ninnies* appeared in 1969, W. H. Auden reviewed it in the *New York Times*. Although he hails the book as a "minor classic," he almost entirely elides discussion of the novel's collaborative production. The bulk of his commentary focalizes the presence of food in the novel: "it is great fun," he writes, "to read about [the characters'] gastronomic experiences: hunger is, after all, a more basic passion than sex." Critical reception of more recent collaborative publications—Forrest Gander and John Kinsella's *Redstart*, or G. C. Waldrep and John Gallaher's *Your Father on the Train of Ghosts*—remains confined largely to the independent literary circuit. By contrast, Gander's *Be With*—primarily authored by Gander, but which contains a collaborative series of poems and photos—received the Pulitzer Prize. This circumscribed market has not prevented poets from adopting collaborative projects, but it has limited the publication of many collaborative works to shorter projects, most of which appear in less commercial and less visible forms, such as the chapbook or the literary journal, or tucked within the pages of a larger manuscript.

* * *

In these collaborative publications, subjectivities seamlessly blend. Philip Schaefer and Jeff Whitney, for instance, have composed two chapbooks of rigorously collaborative poems: *Radio Silence*, which won the 2014 Black River Chapbook Competition and was released from Black Lawrence Press in 2016, and *Smoke Tones*, released in 2014 from the now defunct Phantom Books. In each of these projects, the voice feels singular, defined. The language stems from what at least appears as a discrete self. Yet most of the poems carefully avoid speaking in the first-person singular. "Static Wound," from *Radio Silence*, begins in the passive voice, its grammatical subject obscured: "There is a silence as old / as silence" (1–2). It continues by directing the reader's attention toward other objects, mostly ones that hover in a marginal space between nature and culture: roadsides, drains, medians, and so forth. The speaker states, "A dead blue jay / flat against a road, sewage / drain where its heart / used to metronome" (2–5). The poem shifts to the imperative—"Think blood as the past life / of red" (17–18)—and only ever engages the grammatical first-person in the plural, at a point in the poem where readers have largely lost track of who is speaking. Even here, its emergence is brief. The "we" performs no direct action: "All we clamor for— / a shot at being happy, / a few wars to learn what / we love" (19–22). The speaker "clamor[s]," yes, but it (they?) does not perform that action in the present.

"Vivisecting" similarly avoids the first-person until its final stanza. The poem begins, "The first out is the heart, small / gourd pulled from a wet pocket / of the body" (1–3). When it does appear, the action of the plural speaker is more distinct. It "dance[s]" and "hop[es]" and "learns" in ways that draw upon and impact its surroundings:

> This is the madness we dance for
> hoping like fire to learn
> the world the way a sloth learns
> a tree's particular curve,
> to come apart piece by
> bloodied piece knowing nothing
> goes back, to call home
> the difficult weather, the severed
> soul, the ball-to-glove thud
> of figs in summer falling
> each morning to mulch.

Even here, one clause extends from another, layering the syntax such that, again, readers lose track of the subject. The "we" "hop[es] . . . to learn," but also "hop[es]" "to come apart piece by / bloodied piece" and "to call home / the difficult weather." As the syntax extends, the subordinate clauses relate more distantly to that initial subject and verb, such that "the severed soul" and "the ball-to-glove thud / of figs" tie more closely to the action of "call[ing] home." By poem's end, readers have largely forgotten the lyric subject—and all the better, as we are charmed by this effusion of compelling and finely wrought images. While the poem avoids the first person, it does not eschew close visual perspective. Rather, its imagistic and even ecological observation focalizes elements of the environment, the apperception of which might contradict the poem's vocal plurality. In other words, Schaefer and Whitney trouble their lyric speaker, whose subjectivity hovers in a space between the one and the many.

A similar effect occurs in Simone Muench and Jackie K. White's *Hex & Howl*, a collaborative chapbook also published by Black Lawrence Press. (Black Lawrence has something of a corner on the collaboration market!) Rare is the "I" in what Ryo Yamaguchi describes as these "intensely sonic poems," whose frequent verbal play veers from "rhyme" to "homophone, assonance, alliteration," and "driving metrical units" (Harriet). These by turns un- or partially rhymed sonnets largely elude internal narration. Instead, they work from the outside, speaking primarily in a singular third- rather than plural first-person: "She's silk static / and wetsuit smooth. / A shawl of dark water, / opaque glass" (1–2, "Portrait as Landscape: Shell Game"). There is an "I" in "Disclosure," but interestingly, that "I" is not the grammatical subject—or rather, it is, but it appears within a monologue, spoken by a third-person subject: "The dress says I will frame your beauty / when I bury you. The dress is a chateau / of ghosts demanding don't go" (1–3). The "dress" speaks, and the "I" is contained within that speech. This is not the case in the title poem, which also commences the book's first section. The poem begins in the second person, "You studied the orange girls" (1), only to position the addressee against a distinct first-person utterance: "I looked through the eyes / of chameleons, the nightmare houses they / inhabited with crystalized skins" (3–5). Assuming readers enter the text with knowledge of its collaborative authorship, one might read the poem's oscillating grammatical subjects, its "You" and its "I," as representing competing subjectivities. In that sense, the poem's dual authors depict an embattled speaker—a subject in conflict with itself. Here, troubled subjectivity becomes more explicit than in Schaefer and Whitney, but it does not disrupt the careful balance Muench and White strike throughout the volume. Rather, it offers yet another vantage through which *Hex & Howl* explores the complicated nature of its collaborative authorship, of which subjectivity and speakership are but a part.

* * *

Not all collaborations consist of dual poetic authorship. Forrest Gander and Michael Flomen's "Littoral Zone" is an ekphrastic collaboration comprised of poems and photographs. The piece appears in *Be With*, an elegiac collection that explores the loss of C. D. Wright, Gander's partner over many years, as well as the act of caring for and grieving his ailing mother, who in her later years suffered from Alzheimer's. Throughout the book, Gander represents and eschews subjectivity, exploring, as Lotte L. S. suggests, the "(in)ability" of his own lyric speaker "to translate its subjectivities." The book is filled with gaps and silences. So much is communicated by what remains unspoken. This is true, too, of Flomen's photographs, whose monochrome textures mobilize shadow and exposure to depict the careful margin between absence and presence. The images are created by dipping photosensitive paper in forest waterways, in Flomen's native Canada. Because they are not produced with a lens, the images do not represent the eye—and therefore, not the "I"—of their maker. Rather, they recreate the textures of their environments, themselves teeming with agencies and subjectivities, none of which are the artist's own.

This is less true of Gander's poems which, though fragmentary, maintain a looser relation to accidence. At the start, there is no "I," not even a "we." The verse speaks rigorously in the third person, describing nonhuman, mostly nonsentient bionts. Drawing on Gander's background in geology, the language is rigorously scientific, and for that reason, it dons the guise of objectivity: "They cruise white mesas moored in night, bumping opalescent dripstone.

Cave onyx. No apparent source of light." Each poem is comprised of three distinct textual modalities: 1) a relatively straightforward prose section, which utilizes almost strictly empirical language; 2) an italicized or partially italicized middle section, itself usually comprised of prose; and 3) a versified final section, which sometimes veers toward subjective, and often more explicitly emotional, expression. The first of these verse sections reads:

> Suspiration from our
> lung-thicket. Lengths of
> limbs in limbo on
> the furrowed sheets:
> so love buds again, a-
> gain in trembles above
> this earth-smoke.

In these lines, Gander introduces only a shadowy first person: a plural subject ("our") whose action he depicts in fragments, never through complete clauses. These observations evince a human presence. The speaker metaphorically associates movement with "Suspiration"—*breathing*—ensconced in "limbs" with "furrowed sheets," an expression of (re)emergent "love." The language is not objective; it is erotic.

Later, these sections adopt the first person directly:

> *Fuegos fatuos*: we cast
> double shadows in Pantone
> blacks. My salamandrine
> longing stutter-caught
> on your nocturnal gorges.
> Until you're sub-
> tracted from the visible
> escarpment and I'm a throbbing
> waste-heap of ghost.

Once again, Gander interprets the debris in Flomen's image, this time as *fuegos fatuos*, what in English we call "will-o'-the-wisps." Here, the speaker describes their appearance in this artificial medium—colored in ink, manufactured by Pantone, LLC—to his own agency, or perhaps to the plural agency of himself and his collaborator, or even to human agency more generally. The referent is unclear, but its subjective plurality (again, "we") is indisputable, slipping later into the singular: "I'm a throbbing / waste-heap of ghost." The effect is elegiac: a spectral absence-presence permeates both image and poem. In this sense, the collaboration, this work of multiple hands, conjures a subjectivity seemingly absent from the poem. We could read it as Wright, or Gander's mother, or another presence entirely, but whatever it is, this presence permeates the image-text pairing, revealing yet another form of collaborative possibility.

* * *

While recent collaborations present various subjective models, poetic form has been doing this for a long time. In fact, many now familiar poetic forms locate their origin in collaboration. Perhaps the most prominent example is the haiku, which began as part of a Japanese call-and-response form called the renga. In the renga, one poet composes a stanza, itself comprised of seventeen *on*, a phonetic unit similar to the English syllable. Anglophone approximations of the form utilize the familiar 5-7-5 syllabic pattern. In the renga, however, a second poet would compose the following stanza, comprised of seven *on* per line, or fourteen *on* in total. Together, the two poets create a tanka, a collaborative verse unit, which can only be forged through the participation of multiple makers. In some iterations, the first poet would begin the following stanza, followed yet again by another stanza composed by the second poet. The result here is an oscillating effect well tooled for argumentation: one poet offers an assertion, which the second poet complicates or refutes. The first poet then takes this assertion up again, or offers a novel train of thought. But as Robert Hass observes, classical renga utilized a "decidedly unwestern" pattern: these poems introduce a third poet, who composes the third stanza, followed yet again by a fourth poet, who composes a fourth stanza and completes the second tanka (299). In this sense, the renga becomes a distinctly social form, which requires the participation of many creative minds. Indeed, renga were composed at parties, often as a form of competition. As one mind builds upon another, revealing its own priorities and observations, the renga shifts, in both tone and subject matter. The result is a poetic exchange, which meanders in the mode of conversation.

Because the renga is capable of broadly collective authorship, it is remarkably well suited to subjects of communal or even national import, a fact evidenced in *Renga for Obama*, a project curated by Major Jackson for the *Harvard Review*. Here, 268 American poets, writing between January 21 and April 30, 2017, composed a single poem celebrating the presidency of Barack Obama—and mourning the inauguration of Donald Trump. Like the traditional renga described above, the poem meanders, emotionally ranging from accomplishment to relief to, unsurprisingly, frustration and fear. The opening tanka, composed by Robert Pinsky and Carol Muske-Dukes, reads:

> Healing in winter
> Lava-flower tea—its wood
> Endures like laurel.
>
> Island-born, cool lava-bloom.
> You. Presiding, laurel-crowned.

Such lines elevate the accomplishments of this unlikely presidential candidate, whose name, birthplace, and experience in 2008 exuded a global ethos much missing from the previous administration. The poem swerves toward humor, as in the January 27 contribution by Tom Sleigh and John Skoyles:

> Nobody said *fuck*
> *you* like he did—a razor
> nick quick as his smile
>
> Romantic, dialectic—
> yet a middle finger too.

And, in the February 18 entry, composed by Jorie Graham and Henri Cole, it becomes elegiac:

> Palmyra destroyed,
> I couldn't talk a whole day.
> Frond-slaps in dry wind.
>
> Switchblade Trump messing with us.
> Please come back when you are strong.

Though the various tanka speak upon a singular subject, the result is a textual fabric as varied and circuitous as anything represented in the canon of classical renga. Though the thought represented throughout the poem can vary widely, the voices speak in unison, expressing with near unanimity their admiration for the eponymous subject and disdain for the incoming administration.

If the renga represents a constitutively collaborative poem, the haiku is forged by the absence of other people. As stated above, haiku begins as the opening movement of the tanka, the call portion of the renga's call-and-response severed from the completed form. A haiku, then, is a solitary cry: a call into silence, to which only silence returns. At first glance, one might wonder how any form could be better tooled to solitary observation. The haiku's brevity, paired with its "cut," or *kireji*, renders it especially amenable to precise lyric utterance. As a "text" in the Barthesian sense, such a form is collaborative, since to be a text even a haiku must find a reader. (The call reaches someone, even if that someone never verbally responds.) As a work, however, haiku seems remarkably singular. Yet even here, the collaborative roots of the form remain operative. One feels the solitude of haiku precisely because of the form's dependence on response, itself made possible through collaboration. Thus when Bashō states, "The squid seller's call / mingles with the voice / of the cuckoo," readers familiar with the renga would expect another poet to complete the tanka. Solitude rings clear not because of the details themselves, but because the form manifests inherent lack. The same is true of Buson: "A bat flits / in moonlight / above the plum blossoms." Other factors contribute: the careful use of enjambment, the precision of the observation, the rich semantic play. But ultimately, such forms gesture toward a receiver, patiently awaiting an answer that will never come. In this sense, even a solitary form is ultimately collaborative, if only through the historical vestiges of its formation.

* * *

In this sense, one might argue that all poetic forms are collaborative, inasmuch as they make use of convention to manipulate their readers' expectations. "Convention" stems from the Latin *convenire*, to "gather" or to "come together." It indicates an assemblage of individual subjectivities into a collective body: a meeting, a network, a mesh. Over time, the repetition of specific styles or techniques accumulate, and through that repetition their use adopts the value of a rule. This is as true of the sonnet as it is of the ghazal, the villanelle, or the pantoum, all of which contemporary poetry inherits from far-flung and often very social circumstances. Scholars believe the sonnet in particular was siphoned off as a stanza from a much longer verse form, perhaps an oral or improvisatory one performed by medieval troubadours. Its earliest iterations appear in the court of the Sicilian King Frederick II, passed like lovers' notes from poets to their potential beloveds. This movement from an oral to a written tradition likely represents a marked shift in the sociality of the form, which as part of a *chanson* would have been intensely communal. As it moves toward this more consolidated style, the sonnet adopts the trappings of lyric utterance. This history is largely speculative, since the earliest sonnets have mostly been lost. By the time it rises to popularity, with the sonnets of Dante and Petrarch, its generic conventions—its pursuit, its rhetoricity, its elaborate conceits—already represent a well-worn form.

Yet the sonnet continues to develop, not least of all as it arrives in English. As many readers have noted, the English language contains a dearth of rhyming words, especially compared to Romance languages. Hence when Thomas Wyatt and Henry Howard, earl of Surrey, devise the first English sonnets, they introduce new rhyme schemes. Wyatt in particular introduces a final couplet and meters his sonnets according to English custom. In short, these poets altered the richly intricate Italian to better suit the limitations of their native tongue. Spenser and, later, Shakespeare will take up these alterations, introducing changes of their own. What today we call the English or, worse, the "Shakespearean" sonnet, is really a transhistorical collaboration, passed through the hands of Petrarch, Wyatt, Surrey, Spenser, Shakespeare, and the host of later poets, from John Keats to Claude McKay. The form readers recognize today was generated through this participatory process. Others take up the form as well, abandoning the quintessentially English couplet. In an effort to elevate English as a literary language, though perhaps also to distance his subject matter from that of his English predecessors, John

Milton makes use of the distinctly Italianate form, harkening back to Dante and to Petrarch rather than to Spenser or Shakespeare. Phillis Wheatley composes the vast majority of her highly rhetorical poems in Popian couplets, some of which, at the length of fifteen lines, take the form of sonnets. In the nineteenth century, John Clare and Percy Shelley fashion their own departures. Ralph Waldo Emerson even composes a prose sonnet, though he does not publish it during his lifetime, and of course, the twentieth-century American sonnet features a wide array of approaches and styles, all of which hover in loose relation to the form's otherwise very prescriptive conventions. My point here is not to adumbrate the long history of the sonnet so much as to demonstrate that, as varied as the sonnet might be today, how crucially even that form relies upon the convention—the coming together, and in that sense, the collective labor—of many agencies and subjectivities, over vast periods of time. While the sonnet is somewhat unique among anglophone forms, its history is not dissimilar from the haiku, the ghazal, the quasida, and many other global verse forms, all of which are forged by such transhistorical, and sometimes, translinguistic collaboration.

* * *

These are a few of the many forms collaboration might take, each of which provides another vantage, a turn of the glass, on the history and practice of creative co-laboring. In this final turn, however, I am reminded of the etymology of the term "community," which stems from the familiar Latin *com*, meaning of course "together," and the root word *munis*, meaning to be "bound" or "under obligation," usually under obligation to a service. In a sense, to be communal means to "build together," but more specifically, it means to be bound, locked, or obliged to participate in such collectivity. This in turn reminds me that no matter how solitary our writing practice may at times seem, no matter how isolated or subjective our lyric speakers, to write and to read is to participate in a collectivity that extends well beyond the page. Sometimes this collectivity manifests as inspiration, a metaphorical *breathing* of ideas into the mind of a reader. We are all familiar with the truism that writing, especially powerful writing, can inspire our readers, as well as with the argument—which I find increasingly thin—that literature can inspire social change. In some cases it can, and has, though I do not think this is or necessarily should be the aim of poetry, at least not of all poetry. As one of my students recently observed, "Sometimes you have to eat your vegetables, and sometimes you get to have candy." Poetry can be candy, too, and maybe that plays a role, maybe even an important role, in our collective being. Wallace Stevens argued that poetry is escapism "in the non-pejorative sense" (402), by which he means that poetry allows us to exit the harshness of the world and reenter it cleansed, able to bear its terrible burdens just a little bit longer. This strikes me as an especially social role of poetry, of all art really, and one of the principal reasons we are bound to labor together, even when some of that creative co-labor results in candy poetry.

But I am also reminded that to compose poetry in any capacity—to practice the literary arts at all—is to engage in a community of readers and writers who came before us and who practice in our midst. No writing occurs in a vacuum, and as we write, we commune—together, we build—a great mesh of works that speak in and through one another. This grand and interconnected body of poetry represents an obligation we share toward one another and the responsibility we hold toward one another's writing. Of course, as Barthes reminds us, these connections are imperfect, for as much as the work represents a specific signification, without a reader it remains a mere "material vestibule" (59), a cold and inactive emblem of the meaning that might be. Our practices as writers are bound together precisely because works need readers, because, without readers, there are no texts.

Of course, the body poetry is not the body politic, and we need not confuse the two. But if our poems are formed by the anticipation of a reader, and are shaped at least indirectly by those readers' expectations, then writing itself is never a solitary act. Even in its most solitary moments, even when the poem produced is difficult, alienating, or hermetic, to write a poem is to participate in an intense act of communal solidarity, one sustained over centuries and across languages, oceans, and national and ideological boundaries. I am not saying that the reading or writing of poetry can come anywhere close to saving the world. Rather, I mean that to practice the art of poetry is, like being itself, to enter into a complex relation of making and being made, and that bound as we are within this sphere, our willingness to repeatedly enter into that relation—to compose poem upon poem—represents an effort toward the radically collaborative creativity that might imagine new forms and novel futures.

Prompt: Write a Social Poem

In the markedly social tradition of the renga, this prompt asks you, first, to gather people together, and is designed with the holiday season in mind (though it might easily be adapted to a summer barbecue or other occasion). Prior to writing, be sure to roast a bird or other festive treat. This might be a turkey or a goose, ideally locally sourced. (If you are vegetarian, tofurkey may suffice!) I recommend assembling a host of holiday beverages. For pairing with poultry, select a pinot noir, but cocktails, champagne, or nonalcoholic mocktails can serve as alternatives. Be sure, too, to obtain a notebook or long sheet of paper. The physicality of the work is important here.

Step 1: Everyone should sit in a circle, ideally around a table with shared food.

Step 2: Select a volunteer, who will compose an opening stanza. This person may compose in haiku (5-7-5) or another syllabic form, or may generate a free-verse stanza. The important thing is that it should be short, only about three lines.

Step 3: Pass the paper to the right, allowing the next person in the group to compose a second stanza, of two lines. In the style of the renga, this may be a 7-7 syllabic stanza. It may consist of two free-verse lines. The poet may also employ another stricture, as they see fit.

Step 4: Again, pass the paper to the right, and permit a third poet to compose yet another stanza. If you are aiming to compose a renga, compose another 5-7-5 syllabic stanza (haiku). If not, compose a three-line stanza of free verse.

Step 5 until the end: Pass the paper again, allowing another poet to compose yet another two-line stanza. Repeat this pattern around the circle for a total of eight stanzas and revisit the poem produced.

Continue writing until the party is finished or until the group feels satisfied with the final product. Depending on how long the piece is, the group might consider workshopping the poem—or leave it as is to represent the spontaneity of conversation and social gathering.

Works Cited

Ashbery, John, and James Schuyler. *A Nest of Ninnies*. Champaign, IL: Dalkey Archive, 2008.

Auden, W. H. "A Nest of Ninnies; by John Ashbery and James Schuyler." *New York Times*, 4 May 1969.

Barthes, Roland. *The Rustle of Language*. Trans. Richard Howard. New York: Farrar, Strauss, and Giroux, 1986.

Donnelly, Timothy. "Dream of a Poetry of Defence." *The Cloud Corporation*. New York and Seattle: Wave, 2010.

Gander, Forrest. *Be With*. New York: New Directions, 2018.

Hass, Robert, ed. *The Essential Haiku: Versions of Bashō, Buson, & Issa*. Hopewell, NJ: Ecco, 1994.

Jackson, Major, ed. *Renga for Obama*. Cambridge, MA: Harvard Review, 2017.

L. S., Lotte. "The Possibilities of Poetry: On 'Be With' By Forrest Gander." *The Quietus*, 23 September 2018.

Marx, Karl. *Capital*, vol. 1. Trans. Samuel Moore and Edward Aveling. Moscow, USSR: Progress Publishing, 1887.

Muench, Simone, and Jackie K. White. *Hex & Howl*. New York: Black Lawrence Press, 2021.

Schaefer, Philip, and Jeff Whitney. *Radio Silence*. New York: Black Lawrence Press, 2016.

Stevens, Wallace. *Letters of Wallace Stevens*. Ed. Holly Stevens. New York: Knopf, 1966.

Thomson, James. *The Seasons*. Ed. James Sambrook. Oxford and New York: Oxford University Press, 1986.

Wordsworth, William. "Preface." *Lyrical Ballads*. Ed. R. L. Brett and A. R. Jones. London and New York: Routledge, 2008. 287–314.

Yamaguchi, Ryo. "Hew & Howl." Harriet Books. 24 August 2021.

STOP, COLLABORATE, AND LISTEN

Traci Brimhall

How

For years I taught advanced poetry workshops in the conventional method: students share work, everyone comments on craft, and the cycle repeats over and over again. But one semester, a messy travel itinerary created a disastrous schedule: a giant hole in our time together. Necessity created an opportunity to change the way I approached my classroom. Rather than get a substitute instructor to patch the hole, I thought about what I most wanted them to do with one another, and came up with the idea of a series of collaboration quests. I often love what great attitudes and close readings students bring to poems, particularly poems that engage in forms of pop culture of their generation, and I wanted to encourage that play and community when I wasn't around, so I created "Multi-Player: A Community Quest."

I call my assignments quests because rather than the dreary connotations of the word "assignment," I want my students to associate the work for class with the risks and play an adventure often requires. I serve as their nonplayer character, or NPC in gamer language, who assigns their quests and sets them off on their journeys for poems. My collaboration quests have three "known" adventures on campus during class time with rules created by me, followed by three "unknown" adventures that the students design for themselves that usually take place off campus on their own schedule.

Why

Many other art forms engage in collaboration. Dance, music, and theater could all be solo features, but most often conversation, engagement, experimentation, and feeding off another person's creativity and energy is a part of these art forms. Even if an art form can be practiced alone, some of the other benefits of collaboration are: learning about someone else's creative practice, being pushed out of one's own comfort zone, and attempting to achieve something one likely wouldn't achieve on their own. It also builds connection among peers, which hopefully continues to benefit the classroom community after the collaborations are over. Additionally, I hoped that by taking the classroom into various locations on campus the experience of collaborations would be more memorable. People tend to remember experiences much more strongly than lectures, so I tried to put my pedagogical values into the prompts I designed for students, creating engagements that would have lasting effects on their writing, thinking, and memories from class.

Structure

It's always helpful to model what you want students to do in an assignment, and even in collaboration, that was no different. I create the first three prompts for students, and they're responsible for designing their next three collaborations. In that first set of prompts, I choose their class partners, and make sure they rotate so they collaborate with and learn from different peers. The prompts I create are often quite specific, though there's room for flexibility and creativity. I tend to create rather directed prompts to ensure that they have guidelines and support to write while doing activities that may feel uncomfortable at first, since they've likely never collaborated in creative writing before. I also try to make the experiences collaborative while having the resultant poems be authored individually, though with some input from the collaborator. Often students are reticent to be co-authors of poems, and it takes some negotiation of artistic boundaries to figure out each person's comfort level. I encourage that step when they design their own prompts and choose their own partners, but in our first round of collaboration, I try and respect the difficulty of learning a new skill and let one part of the process feel familiar, such as individual authorship.

Though I often rotate the activities based on weather or building access, here are some of the prompts I have used in the past to initiate our collaboration quest:

Make Words Dance . . . No, Really: I have students roam the university library together and find a private book stack, choose a song, sync their phones, and dance in the stacks together. These can be slow swaying songs or they can party as hard as their headphones allow. When the song is over, they grab a book close to them, take five words from it, and write. I ask them to begin with how their body feels at rest and record the experience backwards, ending the poem on the wildest or happiest moment of dancing nearly alone with some books.

Mapmaker, Mapmaker, Make Me a Map: My university has a tree walk where numerous signs in front of trees contain both basic information and QR codes that link to further facts about the trees. I ask students to walk the campus paths until they encounter a tree they find interesting, read more about it, then use five words from the information and write about their sensory experiences while walking around and what animal they wish they could transform into.

Portrait of the Artist as ________: In this prompt, I let student pairs choose between visiting the student art gallery or the entomology building, where insect specimens decorate the halls. Pairs walk the gallery or hallways and stop in front of a piece of art or bug that they find captivating and talk about why. Their partner looks up information about that art form or insect and uses those facts to weave in extra details, braiding those external facts with the feelings and memories their peer used to talk about that piece of art or insect.

Lego Love Game: My university's architecture library has a large bin of Legos. When we meet there, students already know they will be building a fantasy structure of their choice while talking to their peer about the person who lives there. I let them know pretty early on while they build that it turns out that their two characters are star-crossed lovers who are separated. Sometimes it's because one lived in a treehouse in the Amazon and another lived in a brick house with no doors, and sometimes it's for other reasons, but alas, their love is not to be. Their prompt is to write the epistolary love poem from one fictional Lego lover to their Lego beloved.

Prompts do not have to be quite as silly as the Lego prompt or require as much mobility and physicality as the tree walk, but when assembling a set of prompts I consider creating a varied approach, ensuring I'm giving students different models of co-creating language, as well as ways to get to know each other that might deepen the relationship without requiring too much personal revelation a student may not want to give.

What's Next

After modeling several forms of collaboration for students, they are invited to choose their next round of partners and design three more collaborations. These often vary wildly, but here are several examples of prompts they wrote for themselves. Often they had different goals and different outcomes, but one of the exciting things about letting each class use their intrinsic motivation to select their own collaboration "quests" in the second round was seeing how diverse the motives and poems turned out to be.

Community: One set of students decided to do their prompts as a group. For one activity, they went to a global foods grocery store and picked out foods they'd never eaten before. They shared the items and wrote poems that used the vocabulary of those foods. The same group also organized a Dungeons & Dragons game together and incorporated the events and language of the game into the poems they wrote afterwards. The great strengths of this style of collaboration are that it revealed a willingness to try new things, and it created experiences among a smaller community within the classroom.

Intimacy: Some students created prompts that deepened their engagement with each other or with strangers. One pair bought flowers together and wrote anonymous encouragement poems, leaving both the flowers and the poems on a car windshield. This pair also shared a lot of information with each other about their pasts and wrote poems to the next person who loved their new friend. Additionally, they both had backgrounds in the visual arts and did a single-line portrait of the other person and wrote a response to the portrait as the other person saw them. These collaborations really went beyond what one could expect in terms of intimacy, but the results were some really moving poems, and it was interesting to see how their poems changed when their audience/reader was a friend they cared about rather than a classroom or a presumed wider audience.

Play: Some collaboration partnerships embrace the unusual, and with the pressures of writing the most deeply personal poems, they embrace the playful side of collaboration. I've seen poetry "cootie catchers," field trips to the zoo, video game sessions, and story dice employed to create dynamic collaborations. While these poems often lack the same pathos of poems in which students are trying to say something more urgent and meaningful, there's a great deal of color and texture to the vocabulary.

Pandemic: I also adapted this assignment during the onset of Covid-19. Since students obviously could not be getting together for these collaborations, I offered prompts of walks and listening to the same song and dancing "together" in their separate shelter-in-place locations. I sent them on virtual trips to art museums for the portrait poems, and encouraged them to still make structures for the "Love Game" prompt, but instead of Legos they could make a blanket fort or something from a cardboard box. They often continued these simplified prompts and would also watch shows together and write poems inspired by those shows, and other self-care and comfort activities often created the moments of inspiration and distant togetherness. While some of these prompts were not as elaborate or creative as those I've seen from students at other times, they did perform the essential function of creating connection and community at a time when students really needed it.

But Are They Learning?

As I often do for many assignments or quests, I ask students to write a reflection about what they learned and from whom they learned the most. While students occasionally say the collaborations won't change the way they approach their own poems, they've never said they didn't learn from the experience. It broadens their sense of what poems can be about and what can inspire them. They end up closer to their peers, and though I haven't conducted any surveys years later to see what students remember most from class, I expect that creating experiences around my pedagogical values imparted memories that endure.

In addition to the broader creative approaches to writing poems, it's also a nice break in the rhythm of the semester to play with Legos or walk among the trees. Although as the quest-giver of class I know some of the takeaways that students will have from this set of collaborations, I am always pleased that there are surprises, that they return from their creative journeys with inside jokes, and a renewed commitment to the classroom community.

OPEN THE HOUSE!
ON COLLABORATION AS COMMUNITY

Dean Rader

1. In Which the Author Confesses to a Profession of Collaboration

Though I think of myself as an introvert and in truth, a stereotypically solitary soul, it has come to my attention that I have spent a great deal of my writing life as a collaborator.

This seems impossible to me.

In my mind, I labor away alone, at my desk or in a library or in an archive or in a museum with, I tell myself, no help from anyone. Every day I stare into the abyss, and the only thing returning my gaze? The vertiginous void. No one is more alone than the writer trying to write, the maker trying to make. The painter before a blank canvas, the sculptor staring at a hunk of granite, the poet, blinking in disbelief at the empty page before her.

And yet, when I look at the spines of the eleven books that bear my name, seven also bear the name of at least one other person. According to my seventh-grade son, that means roughly 77 percent of my books are collaborations. Add to that a series of unique artist books I did with the calligrapher Thomas Ingmire, and that number shoots up over 80 percent.

What's more, my collaborations appear not to be confined to books.

The three most enjoyable and rewarding projects I'm currently engaged in also turn out to be collaborative. To wit: in 2021, the poet Victoria Chang and I began a collaborative poetry review column for the *Los Angeles Review of Books*, called "Two Roads: Poetry in Dialogue," in which we try to upend the traditional monologic and somewhat self-important individual reviewer discourse. Each review is a dialogue in which we talk through our engagement with a book. Also begun in 2021 is a rather random but wholly engrossing project I rather selfishly—*see!?*—titled "Poems that Changed Me." In December 2020, at the end of the most bizarre, violent, tragic year in recent memory, I was thinking about transformation and decided to start a weekly video series in which I posted a video of me reading and discussing a poem that had changed me as a writer, a teacher, a scholar, a husband, a father, a person. To my great astonishment, I completed this project, but as someone pointed out, these too are a form of collaboration. The videos are a demonstration of how one person interacting with one text produces a third experience. Without knowing it, these videos were collaborations with Wallace Stevens or Jorie Graham or Rita Dove or Rainer Maria Rilke or LeAnne Howe or Ada Limón or Terrance Hayes. In 2022, I took this one step further and invited other poets, writers, and editors to post videos of themselves talking about transformative poems, thereby extending the cooperative framework to 52 other writers collaborating with a host of other poets.

However, my most immersive and most obsessive recent collaboration is with the artist Cy Twombly. For the last two years, I have been writing poems that enter into conversation with Twombly's drawings and paintings, many of which signify as poetry or literally include poetry. Frequently, his "pictures" feature scribbled lines by poets like John Keats, Sappho, Federico García Lorca, Stephane Mallarmé, and Rainer Maria Rilke. Sometimes, his works are nothing more than the word VIRGIL or ORPHEUS written by hand on paper. These pieces require double decoding of both "drawing" and "writing"— and ask, subtly, if there is even a difference between the two. I want to believe (and do) that Twombly saw these intertextual engagements as collaborations. He illustrates scenes from *Iliad*, edits George Seferis, and even co-authors a book with the Mexican poet Octavio Paz in the gorgeous *Octavio Paz, Eight Poems, Cy Twombly, Ten Drawings*. I see Twombly's art as an invitation to interact. To be more specific, I see it as an invitation to co-create. This is done on the interpretive level in terms of reading my way into his texts—let's call them texts—but also as a fellow artist, I feel called to be the bridge back to poetry. So much of his work is an interaction with the lexical in much the same way mine is an interaction with the visual. Twombly collaborates with Rilke, I collaborate with Twombly. The chain, the circle, the cycle continues.

2. In Which the Author Reveals His Confession Is Also His Thesis

My point is that collaboration takes many forms. We collaborate all the time: when we sing along with a song, when we build a Lego ship with our kids, when we edit another person's essay, when we write a poem about a dead poet, when we cook a meal with our spouse, when we garden, when we mount an exhibition, when we tutor, when we engage in group therapy, when we play an instrument, when we write a letter, when we create a meme, when we translate a poem, when we help the checker bag our groceries. In many ways, art is itself a history of human collaboration with the collective unconscious, the symbols and echoes of our culture, our dreams, anxieties, tragedies, and traumas. In short, we are all, many times a day, collaborating.

I would like to take this notion of macro collaboration, fold it into a paper airplane, and fling it around the room of this essay to see if it can fly. Or, put a different way, I would like to suggest that thinking more broadly about collaboration is a good way not only to assist the individual artist make work. Equally important is that engaging in collaborative practices is an excellent way to build community.

3. In Which the Author Expands upon His Claim that Collaboration Can Foster Community

I tend to think of community in two ways. One is the more conventional notion of community as a large group of people living and/or working together. Most of us agree on this definition or understanding of community. It might be a town, it might be an office, it might be a nonprofit group, it might be a book club, it might be a social organization. I'm also interested in a more invisible or at least less tangible community that might be best described as an historical community or an aesthetic community. By this I mean the lineage of authors or artists or activists that our own practice connects us to. *Community* comes from the Latin *communis*, which means "common, public, general, shared by all or many." I love this last phrase—"shared by all or many." It is in this way that our individual artistic practice is a way of forming and participating in community. Poetry is a community that is shared by many. Millions of people have engaged in the act of composing (horrifically embarrassing) poems; so, when we do that, we participate in one of the longest and oldest communities. When we play the cello, when we paint an abstract painting, when we sing into our phones, we do so in the sunset of countless billions before and in the predawn of those after us. We think so often that art happens in solitude (see my opening confession), when in reality it takes place in community. Our shared endeavors, our shared failures, our shared yearnings for articulation are as old as language itself.

The story critics and historians like to tell about Emily Dickinson is that she wrote in isolation and that she wrote for herself. But I have never believed that. One time, I told my students that a scholar uncovered proof that Dickinson's dashes were really blanks—spaces where she wanted to put words but could not. I retyped the poems and replaced the dashes with blanks and made the students put words where the blanks are. Without knowing it, my students became co-authors with Emily Dickinson.

I think she would have approved.

When I read her work, I sense in it an extension. I feel her reaching out, trying to communicate. By the way, *communication* and *community* share a root; so, the very act of communicating is always already the act of community building. And in Dickinson's poetry, there are endless moments of connection in which we feel the sense of *address*. We know we are being spoken to:

> I've none to tell me but to thee
> This—would be Poetry— / Or love—the two coeval come
> The spreading wide my narrow Hands / To gather paradise
> Oh March, Come right upstairs with me— / I have so much
>   to tell—
> If I can stop one heart from breaking, / I shall not live in vain;
> I'm Nobody! Who are you? / Are you—Nobody—too? /
>   Then there's a pair of us!
> This is my letter to the World

I could go on, but even in the most reclusive of writers, there is a desire for community; but more importantly, an enactment of community. We see this brilliantly in "[I think I was enchanted]," her poem about discovering and devouring the work of Elizabeth Barrett Browning. She describes reading Browning as a "Jubilee" and suggests that the poet's writing and her reading create a kind of fellowship. Here, Dickinson collaborates with Browning, and in our reading of her reading, we collaborate with her—and by extension with Browning.

The joyful, celebratory tone of this poem—almost one of ecstasy—is impossible to miss. That sense of glory, I believe, emanates from the fact that Dickinson is placing herself in Browning's line. She contextualizes her own poetry with her predecessor's. The ecstasy comes in the knowledge of that poetic lineage, that writerly circle. The importance of being admitted to that community makes me think of one of my favorite passages in all of literature. In canto IV of *The Inferno*, Virgil leads Dante into a section of Limbo, where he sees the great poets Ovid, Lucan, Horace, and Homer talking among themselves. Imagine coming across your four poetic mentors in the same place at the same time, while being guided by your supreme poetic mentor, Virgil. And then imagine this happens:

> So I saw gathered at the edge of light
> The masters of that highest school whose song
> Outsoars all others like an eagle's flight.
>
> And after they had talked together a while,
> They turned and welcomed me most graciously,
> At which I saw my approving Master smile.
>
> And they honoured me far beyond courtesy,
> For they included me in their own number,
> Making me sixth in that high company.

Oh, the pure joy of being invited into "their own number." The affirmation of inclusion in that community! To make art is to partake in the greatest and oldest community.

4. In Which the Author Pivots and Discusses Art and More Conventional Modes of Community

Not all of us will experience what Dickinson did when she invited herself into Browning's company or what Dante felt when he was invited into that of Horace, Homer, Ovid, Lucan, and Virgil. Or even what I feel when I insinuate myself into the conversation Twombly is having with Rilke while Rilke is having a conversation with the infinite (though I have to say I do love being in the "high company" of Twombly and Rilke.) Side note: during the dark days of the Covid-19 pandemic shutdown in San Francisco, I acquired a signed copy of Rilke's book about Auguste Rodin. It was an extravagant purchase for me, but the correspondences were too strong to ignore. Here was a book Rilke, a poet, wrote about a visual artist while he was trying to find his own voice. And here I was, a poet, writing about another visual artist (Twombly), while also trying to find a voice for this project. Add to that the experience of touching Rilke's signature, of holding a book he held (that maybe Rodin also held). Somehow, I felt like something was being passed down from him to me.

But I digress.

What I want to say here is that collaborative enterprises do not only create but build community.

For example, in my poetry workshops, I always have my students write collaborative poems. How they do this varies from assignment to assignment (see the exercises at the end of this chapter for more detail). But two remarkable things always emerge. One, and least important (but not insignificant), is that these are often the best poems the students produce over the course of the semester. Second is how much fun the students have working together to make their poem. Neither one wants to let the other down, so they take the project seriously because even more is at stake. It is not just about their reputation as a poet but about their reputation as a partner, a human.

One of my favorite exercises is a kind of chain poem that we write as an entire class. Here, all the students begin with a blank piece of paper on the desk. They each write one word on the paper and then pass it to their neighbor. That person writes one word in response to the first word and then passes it along. And so forth and so on until everyone in the class has written at least one word on every poem. If there are 20 students in the class, at the end of the exercise, we will have 20 poems of 20 words.

Now, there are some interesting decisions each of the collaborators must make. When do I start a new stanza? How should I set up the person following me? As we are clearly getting close to the end, how should I tie up this poem? Do I keep the tone or change things up? Is the poem funny or earnest or experimental or dark or playful? What is my responsibility to the words and patterns that came before me? It is a fascinating project that makes the students both a little anxious and a little excited.

When we are all done, the student reads the poem that they began out loud. It is always surprising to see the turns the poems take as well as how different they all are from each other. Typically, when I do this exercise it has a second component, which I recommend.

Here in San Francisco, we have a wonderful organization called the San Francisco Center for the Book (SFCB), which functions as a community space, a classroom, a museum, and a gallery—all devoted to the art and history of printing and binding. I tell my students that we are going to make a broadside of a class-authored poem. So, after reading all the poems, we vote on the one we want as our class poem. I send that poem to the SFCB, and they prep the poem for broadside printing. On the day of our field trip to the SFCB, the students each get to take turns placing a piece of paper on the press, pulling the lever, and printing a copy of the poem that we wrote as a community. They leave with a gorgeous, professionally produced broadside of their poem.

This simple act does a lot of work.

First, it codifies the poem we wrote as a group. It is literally a published, printed document—often the first such thing for the students. Second, it enables the students to participate in the revered history of printing and printmaking. They get to do what Gutenberg did. Third, it places them in context with the rich tradition of chain poem-making like tanka and renga. The part I love is when they decide—and this seems to happen every time—that they all want everyone's signature on the broadside. Again, the semiotics of community.

One does not need a facility like the SFCB to make something like this happen. You can create a document on a computer, print it out, have everyone sign it, and post it on doors and walls. You can post the handwritten version, both literally on a wall and virtually on social media.

But other projects come to mind.

Once, my friend Brian Clements hosted a huge Walt Whitman project in which he invited writers, musicians, and artists into a room where we all took turns writing our favorite Whitman quote on a giant roll of butcher paper. He then taped it to the wall, so that it wrapped around the entire room, effectively creating Whitman wallpaper. At my son's school, for National Poetry Month, one of the teachers, Megan Adler, herself a fine poet, hung huge pieces of paper up on the wall of the school and asked students to create a group poem by writing one line each. Students would stop on their way to class, read what had been written before them, then add their own line and be on their way.

The options are endless.

5. In Which the Author Expands Even Further but Extraordinarily Briefly on Collaboration and Community

So far, everything I have discussed has been pretty literary, and to be honest, pretty poetry-centric. But similar exercises can be done with visual art, music, prose, singing, and acting. I have some ideas about how one might conduct these experiments, but I do not want to be bossy. I am nervous about overdetermining how one might go about organizing something for a field of interest I know less about. So, I feel like it might be best to transition to a section

6. In Which the Author Returns to His Own Collaborative Projects in a Perhaps Naïve but Optimistic Belief that the Personal is a Portal to the Communal

I confess that in an essay on collaboration and community, I fear I have spent too much time discussing my own collaborations. But I have found that while many of us want to collaborate, we don't always know how, and we don't always see examples of successful collaborations. Since this book is designed to be a practical guide with techniques for building community, I thought I would provide examples of many different collaborative projects that were successful but also repeatable.

For example, in 2020 my friend Luisa Caycedo-Kimura and I decided to collaborate. We did not know what form our collaboration would take, but we knew we wanted to try something. We landed on the haibun, an ancient Japanese form that pairs prose and poetry. A typical haibun begins with a short bit of prose, often a kind of prose poem, that is followed by a haiku. We decided to write two haibun—one in which Luisa wrote the prose and I follow with the haiku and one in which I began with the prose and she ended with the haiku. We thought the two collaborative haibun might themselves be in conversation with each other so that it could be a collaboration within a collaboration—community within community, conversation within conversation. We wound up being happy with the result and published them in the thirteenth issue of *Diode*.

I tell this story to tell a larger one: collaboration can happen in many ways and take many forms. One of my favorites is the cento. The cento, like the haibun, is a classic poetic form made up entirely of previously existing lines. My friend and collaborator Simone Muench (we wrote an entire book of collaborative sonnets together) has an amazing chapbook called *The Wolf Centos*, in which every single line of poetry in the book comes from another poem. I love this project because each poem is an assemblage of other poets. For example, one 13-line Wolf Cento contains lines from Anne Sexton, Dylan Thomas, Larry Levis, Ingeborg Bachmann, Octavio Paz, Henri Michaux, Agnes Nemes Nagy, Joyce Mansour, William Burroughs, Meret Oppenheim, Mary Low, Adrienne Rich, and Carl Sandburg. Thus, not only is Muench collaborating with all of these poets but they are all collaborating with each other! Carl Sandburg and Adrienne Rich working together! Octavio Paz and Ingeborg Bachmann as poetic partners! It hardly gets any better than this.

I often assign a cento in my poetry workshops, but I also typically assign them in literature classes as well. One of the most successful assignments I have done was in a literature class where students were struggling with Wallace Stevens poems. So, I assigned them a cento. They had to write a 20-line cento with lines from 20 different Stevens poems. I assumed the students would hate the assignment, their poems, me, and worst of all, Stevens, but the opposite was the case. They loved the assignment, and it made them appreciate Stevens, in part because they became co-creators with him. One student even built a web page and published all of the centos. We were all amazed at how the centos made Stevens's work come alive and yet how each cento somehow represented the student's individual perspective. The website merely added to the sense of collaboration and community because it showed us all united in the same endeavor.

When I think about community and collaboration, especially regarding my own work, I always ultimately land on two anthologies I co-edited and how they changed my life. My tone has been light throughout this essay, so you may think I am being arch here, but I assure you I am not.

In 2019, CMarie Fuhrman and I collaborated on what we thought was a groundbreaking book, *Native Voices: Indigenous American Poetry, Craft, and Conversations*. This anthology not only collects poems by 44 different poets from differing schools and generations, but it also pairs those poets with craft essays authored by the poets themselves. This last part is critical to the anthology because they highlight the poems as art. Rather than assuming that contemporary Indigenous poetry is folklore or "culture," *Native Voices* asks readers and writers to look at these poems through an aesthetic lens. But for our purposes here, they demonstrate how Indigenous poems are themselves collaborations with other poets, artists, and makers. We asked the poets to write about a poem or poet that was important to them, and the responses are astonishing in their breadth and depth. I was (and am) particularly taken with the essay by the Nez Perce poet Michael Wasson, in part because it does a kind of triangulation between poetry and art that I am also doing. In his piece, he is filling in the gaps, creating gaps, making a new text through a collaboration with an Eduardo Corral poem that is itself a response to a work of art by Tino Rodriguez. Michael's text is not only textual, it is also visual. It points toward art, it points towards semiotics, it points toward language, it points toward the self, it points toward the Nez Perce, it points back at us.

The poems in *Native Voices* exhibit superb talent and unrivaled vision. They reflect both traditional and cutting-edge uses of language, line break, white space, fragmentation, repetition, and elision. These are true artists at the peak of their craft. This is not to say the poems are value free. On the contrary. However, these poems don't just address history or land or ceremony; they also take on colonialism, poverty, land rights, Indigenous genocide, sexuality, and cultural loss. Some of the poems are angry. Some are funny. Some are hard to understand. Some are easy to understand. Some ask you to rethink history. Some remake history. This book teaches history and social science through poetry and conversations about poetry. In other words, it collaborates with a totality of forces to make sense of the past and, hopefully, to help carve a new path for the future.

But no project I've done has been as personally transformative as the collection *Bullets into Bells: Poets and Citizens Respond to Gun Violence*, which, again, is a collaborative editing effort with Brian Clements and Alexandra Teague. Here, we pair 50 poems that take on gun violence with responses written by survivors of shootings, activists in the anti-gun violence movement, parents of kids killed by guns, like Tamir Rice's mother, and people who found themselves in the middle of the aftermath, like the ER doctor attending to the victims of the Sandy Hook shooting. Thus, the anthology is a series of 50 collaborations between poetry and prose, between poets and survivors.

Working on this book, traveling around the country doing readings, visiting schools, and doing interviews, opened me up to a series of communities I had only a passing knowledge of or never knew about, including Moms Demand Action, the Peace Center of Connecticut, Faith in Action, Live Free, Theater for Change, Giffords Law Center to Prevent Gun Violence, and dozens of other local support organizations.

My ultimate thesis is that through collaboration I have found not just community but communities. Sometimes those communities are dead poets, but sometimes, that is the community I want. Sometimes those communities are nonprofits and activist organizations, which tend to be the opposite of dead poets, but sometimes, those are the communities I want. But every time, through collaboration, I have found my best aesthetic self. I think I might do my best work when it is contingent, reliant, cooperative.

I have spent most of my life trying to debunk the myth of individual genius. But I don't know that I thought that collaboration would make me make my best art.

But it has.

7. In Which the Author Reveals that Community and Collaboration Are Really about the Same Thing

Listening.

Listening to your partner, to the text, to your neighbor, to your enemy.

Listen to the muse. Listen to language. Listen to what is said and what is not.

When it comes to making art, there is only listening. There is nothing else. When it comes to collaboration, our responsibility is to listen.

Not only that, how we listen is key. We should not listen to respond but to reflect.

I believe that I listened to all of my collaborators.

And art was made, and community was formed.

8. In Which the Author Goes Existential

And so now here we are—writer and reader. Do you feel us collaborating? I am trying to anticipate what you want from me in this final section. You are curious how I am going to end this essay that argues so hard for co-authorship. Where do we go?

In my first book of poems, *Works & Days*, there is a poem called "A Genealogy of Unfinished Love Poems," which features a poem in four parts, with four different titles, but each poem includes several missing words. Blanks, as in a Mad Lib. Readers are invited to fill in the blank so that they co-author the poem along with me. One of my all-time favorite experiences occurred at a reading here in San Francisco. After the reading, I overheard one woman telling her friend this: "I loved that blank love poem. Let's buy the book, go get a bottle of wine, and fill in the blanks."

This essay is full of blanks.

Like my imagined Dickinson poems.

Details I left out.

For some of you, I focused on the wrong things. Sorry. For others, you may have felt invited in, perhaps like now, as I address you directly, admitting my shortcomings.

Are we in community? I like to think so.

Are we collaborating?

If you are reading this, you already know the answer.

9. In Which the Author Provides Some Exercises for Your Collaborative Pleasure

A. In my essay, I mention my collaborations with Simone Muench. Our book, *Suture*, was a collection of collaborative sonnets. And it was collaborative in two ways. First, each sonnet begins with a line from a sonnet by a well-known poet, like Pablo Neruda, Adrienne Rich, Gerard Manley Hopkins, Rita Dove, etc. So, let's say Simone would send me a line from Edna St. Vincent Millay—that would become the first line of the poem. Then I would write three more lines creating our first quatrain. As the first author, I would establish any rhyme pattern or syllable count, as well as the tone, mood, etc. Then, I would send that to Simone, who would write four more lines. Then she would send it to me, and I would write a tercet, or if I was feeling edgy, I would write another quatrain! Then I would send it back to her and she would finish it either Petrarchan style with a tercet or Shakespearean style with a couplet.

I often give my students the same assignment. I put them in pairs and require them to write two sonnets, one that student A starts, and one that student B starts.

B. Assign a renga. A renga is an ancient Chinese chain poem. Sometimes it would include 20 or 30 men and a lot of drinking. So, one option is to get a group of people and agree on a system. Then, simply, start writing and send the poem around the room!

In the late 1970s, four poets from four different countries—Octavio Paz, Jacques Roubaud, Eduardo Sanguineti, and Charles Tomlinson—published a very cool renga in four different languages with an English translation. I like their approach. Find four friends and agree on a system. I like a cycle of four poems of four stanzas each. So that when you are done, you have four poems in which each person has written the first, second, third, and fourth stanza of a poem. In graduate school, I did this with Brian Clements, Paul Dean, and David Chin. We wound up publishing some in a collaborative writing anthology. It was a lot of fun.

C. Write a haibun. Pair up students and require them to write two poems. In the first poem, student A writes the prose section, and student B finishes up with the haiku. Then, student B starts the next poem in prose, and student A completes it with the haiku.

D. Assign an exquisite corpse. This classic prompt from the Surrealist period continues to dazzle. Any number of people can collaborate, but it works well with 10 to 30. Begin with a blank piece of paper, ideally a legal one (the long kind). The first author writes a line of poetry, then folds the paper over, concealing what they wrote from the next person. They write a line, then fold over the paper blocking both and pass it along, each person writing and folding. When you are done, you unfold and read the wacky result. Proponents of the exquisite corpse suggest agreeing on a syntactic pattern so that every line is more or less similar, such as: adjective, noun, verb, adjective, noun. I find this creates monotony. But perhaps giving *some* guidelines is a good idea.

E. The cento. I talk about the cento in the essay. *Cento* is Latin for "patchwork" or "collage." A cento is a poem that is comprised entirely of lines from other poems. I recently wrote a cento that is a series of lines from Rilke's *Duino Elegies* (Stephen Mitchell translation). I like giving myself some limits with centos—only women poets or only Indigenous poets or only Wallace Stevens poems, etc. Peter Gizzi has a fun cento that culls lines from the New York School of poets.

F. My colleague at the University of San Francisco, Peter Novak, is a noted actor and director. He agrees about the role of listening in collaboration. In his acting classes, he does two impromptu exercises that focus on listening. In the first, he lines up eight actors in two rows of four. One person comes up with a title to a story that no one has ever heard of: *Simon Goes Spelunking in South Wales* or *Who Drank My Mint Julip?* Something like that. Then, someone starts telling the story. At any moment, any of the seven other people can just point to anyone else in the group. At that instant, the person telling the story must stop, and the person pointed to has to pick up the story in mid-sentence or even mid-word. Any time someone points to another person, that person must continue the story. To do this, you must be listening carefully and actively. Another favorite is for two people to have a conversation with one caveat. One person begins by asking the other a question. The second person has to begin their answer with a word that begins with the same letter that ended the first person's last word. So, let's say the question is, *"How are you today?"* The second person would have to respond with a word that begins with the letter

Y. *"You know, I'm okay. How are you?"* And the starter would have to begin their sentence with a word that starts with U. *"Unusually sucky, thanks for asking."* Then a g-word and so on . . .

G. Another colleague at USF I love working with is the artist Jenifer Wofford, with whom I team-taught a class on "Making." She begins every class with a 10-minute extemporaneous drawing exercise. She gives her students 10 minutes to draw something based on specific parameters—only octagons or bunnies or realism or only straight lines. Then, when the time is up, everyone is required to share. Often, little bits of data emerge that energize and bond the group.

Works Cited

Clements, Brian, Alexandra Teague, and Dean Rader, eds. *Bullets into Bells: Poets and Citizens Respond to Gun Violence*. Boston: Beacon Press, 2017.

Dickinson, Emily. *The Complete Poems of Emily Dickinson*, ed. Thomas H. Johnson. Boston: Little, Brown and Company, 1960.

Fuhrman, CMarie, and Dean Rader, eds. *Native Voices: Indigenous American Poetry, Craft, and Conversations*. North Adams, MA: Tupelo Press, 2019.

Muench, Simone. *The Wolf Centos*. Louisville, KY: Sarabande Books, 2014.

———, and Dean Rader. *Suture*. Black Lawrence Press, 2017.

Paz, Octavio, and Cy Twombly. *Octavio Paz, Eight Poems, Cy Twombly, Ten Drawings*. Text by Udo Brandhorst. Köln: Udo and Anette Brandhorst, 1993.

———, Jacques Roubaud, Eduardo Sanguineti, and Charles Tomlinson. *Renga: A Chain of Poems*. New York: George Braziller, 1971.

Rader, Dean. *Works & Days*. Kirksville, MO: Truman State University Press, 2010.

TOWARD A THIRD VOICE: COLLABORATION, ARTISTIC RISK, AND CONCEPTUAL PLAY

Chris Campanioni and Kristina Marie Darling

Long before the Internet was rerouted from military servers and mainstreamed, Foucault understood the efficacy of anonymous interactions on the level of literature, imagining "a culture where discourse would circulate without any need for an author." But what he was asking for in "What Is an Author?" is something we can probably better answer today. Because it seems less and less likely (or germane) to call into question the need for an author in a culture in which almost everyone is writing, producing, and reproducing words—and increasingly more effective to think about reevaluating the notion of a single author, or what it means to *write by yourself*. But it isn't enough to say, I am sitting here, alone, at my dinner table that I so often use for writing, as I type this, and yet I'm in constant communication and communion with all of you, so many of whom I will never know. One would have to testify to the particular medium we have at our disposal, the actual discourse of the Internet, its ultimate permissibility, its provocations for collaboration and co-creation. One would have to surrender the idea that authors own anything besides our will to keep producing, and our desire for change; and to modulate means to resist without negating, to alter without omitting, to enable something new to come forward: unfolding of the text into the anonymity of a murmur.

And really it isn't the Internet that has fostered these ideas of collaborative authorship but the classical world. We already know that for the ancients, every act of creation comes from elsewhere, is something unformed or uncompleted, which was *made to grow*. It's why "to author" all the way down to its Latin roots signifies advising, witnessing, *and* transferring. It's why to author something means to also forget the act of saying "I," to forget it or to make it recede into the background in service of the other or others, on behalf of a community, for the sake of an audience.

When I think of collaborative poetics I often think about the poetics of Relation, and about what it means to be directly in contact with everything possible, an always-open structure in which, as Glissant said, "the creator of a text is effaced, or rather, is done away with, to be revealed in the texture of his creation." When a solid melts, it reveals something always underneath, something at the very bottom, something inside—something new and something that was *always already there*. What I want is the intimacy of anonymous encounters within the text itself, and yet to be effaced and revealed, even and especially by my own authorial departure. And it would take the form of a repetition or a reversal; a re: verse in which we correspond lyrically; a re: verse in which our correspondence becomes the poem.

Of course, an integral part of any correspondence is the space between things, those slender apertures lit up with waiting. It is in these liminal spaces that possibility accumulates. We write toward this space, in response to its silences.

* * *

Because we are neither here nor there, the rules of syntax and grammar, and their implicit logic, no longer hold. More specifically, liminal spaces offer the possibility of new causal relationships. Which is to say, *after this* no longer means *because of this*. Since we are in no man's land, working at the periphery of the governing bodies associated with language, it becomes difficult if not impossible to enforce any normative idea about how language, and narrative, for that matter, should behave.

Nota bene: the meaning of the word *aperture* is twofold: 1) a hole or gap; 2) a space through which light passes in an optical or photographic instrument, particularly the variable opening by which light enters a camera.

A collaboration functions in much the same way, capturing radiance as it passes from one person's fingertip to the next.

In a recent interview on their co-written volume, John Gallaher and G. C. Waldrep refer to this interstitial space, and the light that fills its corridors, as the "third voice," belonging to both practitioners and neither one of them. Because there is no textual ownership, per se, it becomes difficult to hold someone accountable, let alone take up the customary practices surrounding language usage: copyright, attribution, citation. It is no coincidence that these routine procedures are bound up with questions of value, and the economies in which texts circulate. By abandoning the single-author text, we create a space outside of (or beyond) the linguistic marketplace.

* * *

One way we can think of this "third voice" is by thinking of glossolalia, this biblical "speaking in tongues" that also represents the generally ungraspable, a polylinguistic discourse that can't be conquered or claimed; that exists, in fact, to disrupt the persistent motion to grasp. And *to grasp* is to understand, but before that, it is the attempt to hold, to have, to own. "How can a living being have language?" Agamben asks. I would return: Is it not, instead, language that has a living being? To the extent that language turns one into an "I" through the act of becoming, a move into subjectification and desubjectification, the unrepeatable and its repetition, within the trauma of enunciation, *so to speak*, or to begin to understand what cannot be spoken. The poetics of collaboration speaks in that silence, that call or signal, coded with repetition and cessation, the pause before another voice returns, a track resumes, a word is placed behind a blinking black dash, if you are doing this at your laptop and we are. And elsewhere—

A message in my inbox provides me WHAT'S NEW IN YOUR GROUP: When does a poem stop being yours? I don't click here to View Discussion; I don't click out. I begin to Add a Comment, which becomes this project, this process of turning off so as to turn the page: a conversation and conversion, but also a returning to the primacy of the event of language, whose power is located in being almost unlocatable. The point is not to know what happens next, as in any good writing, but to take it further; to resist the authorial urge to answer, to close things off, to finish. Part of this is in knowing the unknowable outside the frame; to relish and relinquish what can't be seen by just your own camera eye. To think of the kitchen table when no one is looking—but more than that, to think of the kitchen table when one has photographed the parlor. Another way of saying this: it is always the unsayable that calls one to speak. When there is more than one voice, we must imagine one another's silences as if they are our own.

* * *

The house grows quiet again. We are unsure who is at the door, and who has already passed through the silver gates. In the parlor, there is a single painting displayed on a white wall. A beige canvas that reads:

THIS PAINTING IS A PROPOSAL. I PROPOSE WE MEET ONCE A YEAR UNTIL ONE OF US CAN'T OR WON'T.

Of course, the obvious question: in that year, filled with works and days, where does the mind travel, and with whom?

In the age of virtual reproduction, most collaborations take place over vast expanses of landscape and weather. The voice on the other end of the receiver could be anyone, not just the dark-eyed girl standing in a garden, holding a plucked flower in her profile pic. It is what we don't know, and cannot yet know, that pulls us farther into a forest of bright and burning branches. Here, fact becomes limitation, inscribing the boundaries of what is possible. It is more liberating not to know.

That silence is the struck match, the last light.

Collaborative Exercise: The Braided Narrative in Correspondence

Part 1 (spend 10 minutes here; don't write these out in any order; don't include the questions in your responses. Feel free to mix and shift without distinction)
One thing that happened today
One thing that didn't
One thing that happened in the past
One thing that will happen
One thing that happened in your dreams

Part 2 (spend 10 minutes here, retaining the instructions above)
Two things you know to be true
Two things you know to be not true
Two questions you want to consider
Three moments of sensation

Part 3 (spend another 10 minutes here)
Ask yourself: what would you be doing if you weren't doing what

you are doing right now? (Part of these poetics is **a poetics of preparation.**)

In Correspondence

After writing these responses out, weave them together in an order/arrangement of your choosing. Spend 10 minutes with this. Think cinematically. When to zoom in? When to pull back and show the larger context? Have the liberty to jump-cut into a moment "late" and to leave "early."

If gathering in a room with others, pass your text to the right, and write into the narrative you've just received. After spending 10 minutes inhabiting the narrative you've received, pass the text to the right, and write into the narrative you've just received. After another 10 minutes, pass each text to the center of the room, so each writer can retrieve (or discover) their "original." Recite the new texts.

If gathering in a Zoom room or any other virtual space, everyone will recite their responses after each part is completed. During this time between parts, integrate and resignify at least *one* answer from someone else's Part 1 or 2 or 3. Use these found and borrowed moments as opportunities to detour.

Collaborative Writing Assignment: Call and Response

Choose a collaborator, then separately answer the following questions in a free write:

What don't you know about your chosen collaborator?

Who was your collaborator before this writing assignment began?

If your collaborator had a secret life, what would it be?

Once you've brainstormed for about 10 minutes, using this set of questions as a prompt, let's see how what we don't know can be material for the imagination. Have one collaborator volunteer to start. Then, using the material from the free write, they should write a brief monologue in the voice of the character they have described. The other collaborator should draft a brief poem, monologue, or hybrid text in response. Then, in call-and-response style, complete a sequence that alternates between the two characters and their respective voices.

Collaborative Writing Assignment: The Satisfaction of Incompleteness

Choose a collaborator. Have one writer create a poem or hybrid text that is intentionally incomplete. Did the rest of the text get burned in a house fire? Did the ending of the poem get torn from the book by an angry romantic partner? Did the archivist misplace it? That's for your collaborator to decide.

Once the first writer has handed over the incomplete text, their colleague should fashion a story to explain why parts of the text are missing, erased, or otherwise mislaid. Then, responding to their collaborator's draft, they should find a way to weave that story of absence and incompleteness into the text.

Collaborative Writing Assignment: Experimental and Found Forms

Have one collaborator draft a page of prose. This page can be about anything. A horror story. An anxiety dream. A fictitious narrative. Then, the other writer should create footnotes, endnotes, indexes, appendices, and other marginalia for that page. Then switch roles. Keep trading back and forth until your text and paratexts are complete. How does switching forms influence your approach to voice, storytelling, and the relationship between collaborators?

Works Cited

Agamben, Giorgio. "Literature and Life in Agamben." https://williamwatkin.blogspot.com/2010/05/literature-and-life.html?utm_source=chatgpt.com.

Foucault, Michel. "What Is an Author?" In Donald F. Bouchard, ed., *Language, Counter-memory, Practice: Selected Essays and Interviews by Michel Foucault*. Ithaca, NY: Cornell University Press, 1980.

Gallaher, John, and G. C. Waldrep. "Part 4 of John Gallaher and G. C. Waldrep on Your Father on the Train of Ghosts." www.boaeditions.org/blogs/main/71628869-part-4-of-john-gallaher-and-g-c-waldrep-on-your-father-on-the-train-of-ghosts?srsltid=AfmBOoquJSA1wdBYMlT5mklPC349JNtl6IKdzsMZuDoJwnzRjQdtc2b8&utm_source=chatgpt.com.

Glissant, Édouard. *Poetics of Relation*. Trans. Betsy Wing. Ann Arbor: University of Michigan Press, 1997. https://criticaltheoryconsortium.org/wp-content/uploads/2018/07/edouard-glissant-poetics-of-relation-1.pdf.

PART TWO

Beyond the Boundaries of the Printed Page: Publishing as Activism, the Book as Ledger

THE BOOK AS A FORUM FOR CONVERSATION: LITERARY PUBLISHING AND CULTURAL MEMORY

Kristina Marie Darling

In a recent issue of the *American Poetry Review*, Carol Ann Johnston notes that "The early avant-garde's play with poetic language as visual art grasped the change in poetic emphasis from aural to visual [. . .] The influence of Cubism and Dadaism encouraged poets to see the page as verbal collage." Johnston rightly calls attention to the transformative work of poets like Stephane Mallarme and William Carlos Williams, whose writing questioned—and substantively revised—prevailing ideas about aesthetic pleasure. Yet the seismic shift that Johnston describes encompassed not just writing, but also the book as a physical object. Texts like "A Throw of the Dice," "The Corset," and *Spring and All* questioned our most basic assumptions about typesetting, white space, and the boundaries of the printed page as a unit of meaning.

Three contemporary poets build on the early avant-garde's experimentation with the page as a visual field, offering us collections that expand our sense of what is possible within a bound and printed book. Gracie Leavitt's *Livingry*, Asiya Wadud's *Crosslight forYoungbird*, and Eve L. Ewing's *Electric Arches* share a commitment to language that performs its meaning across the vast expanse of the page. In many ways, these writers' highly performative language calls attention to its own containment—by grammar, by genre conventions, and by the preconceived ideas that readers bring to the book as a cultural artifact. Indeed, Ewing, Wadud, and Leavitt make visible, through their innovative artistic practice, this containment of voices and texts.

As each collection unfolds, we are offered language that breaks boundaries—between the written and the visual arts, between representation and metaphor, between types of aesthetic experience—rendering us suddenly aware of the limitations we impose upon language before it has even begun to unfold before us. For some readers, this presentation of language might be jarring, even irreverent, as we are not used to texts that make their own rules. However, as Ewing herself reminds us, "The space was always there."

* * *

Leavitt's *Livingry* often reads as an exercise in scale. Here, we are offered poems that are slim and tersely lineated, white space overwhelming the texts' seeming smallness. Yet the language in *Livingry* resists this categorization, reacting against any possible description of the writing as diminutive, orderly, or neat. Leavitt invokes textual difficulty as an aesthetic gesture, and the careful withholding of meaning becomes a purposeful part of the reader's experience. In this way, the interplay of the poems' visual appearance and their metaphorical richness, and their relative scale in relation to both the page and the work that's asked of the reader, creates a provocative tension, a spark that ignites the collection.

The poems themselves read as dense soundscapes, as Leavitt eschews the semantic meaning of words in favor of their sonic richness. Reminiscent of Zukofsky's sound-based translations, the poems in *Livingry* challenge our limiting definitions of meaning and coherence, envisioning the poem as a space in which to offer alternative frameworks for thinking, storytelling, and elegizing. She writes, for example, in "Loose Leaf,"

> This morning
> the mystery
> shattered itself, but I
> don't want to
> only ornamentally
> absorb, therein
> sly call perhaps
> to a part and
> separate.

Here Leavitt offers lines that are as charged as they are minimalistic. Though parsed out two or three words at a time, the language in this sonically vibrant, singing poem overwhelms the seemingly small rhetorical space in which it is housed. What's more, as Leavitt transitions from "morning" to "mystery," from "ornaments" to their inevitable "shattering," it is the moments of rupture, the pauses between each measured line, that set off each line's intricate and tangled music. For Leavitt, "to be a part and / separate" is a necessary part of the poem's work, a metaphor for lineation as much as it is for the poem's appearance on the printed page. Leavitt reminds us, subtly and skillfully, that poems are visual compositions, even—or especially—when we fail to realize it.

* * *

Electric Arches expands on Leavitt's consideration of poetry as an inherently visual endeavor. Filled with original artwork, handwritten notes, and poems on black pages, Ewing's poems challenge our culture's fixation on book publication as a way of claiming authority within a linguistic landscape that is inherently unstable. What's striking about Ewing's work is the way she embraces this uncertainty.

Ewing destabilizes, through her provocative visual experimentation, our idea of the book object as finished, static, and not subject to change. By transitioning from typewritten text to handwritten notes and drawings, Ewing questions the way our culture elevates the finished product, while devaluing the processual. Indeed, Ewing places seemingly impromptu notes squarely within a perfect bound book, carving a space for experimentation, improvisation, and play within a form heretofore reserved for language functioning as product and commodity. Ewing writes, for example, in "the first time [a re-telling],"

> This time she screamed at me. "You little nigger! You almost hit me with that bike! Go back to your nigger Jesse Jackson neighborhood!" I told my mom and she told me the flying bike should only be for weekends, but okay, I could use it just this once.

It is important to note that the second half of this passage is handwritten, beginning with "told me the flying bike." For Ewing, breaking free of cultural stereotypes requires reenvisioning the forms of discourse that bear oppression into the world, that give injustice its form and structure. The transition to handwritten notes, then, becomes politically charged, as Ewing gestures at a version of personal and shared history that could be opened to substantive change, strike-throughs, and revisions.

In addition, Ewing reveals the book object, and the textual economies in which it circulates, as being bound up in existing mechanisms of power in our culture. She provocatively challenges the ways we assign value to language, as one tends to revere finished, typeset, bound product over the artifact of its process. For Ewing, process is where the possibility lies, since in this liminal space, the rules with which we are familiar no longer hold.

* * *

Wadud's *Crosslight for Youngbird* blends hybrid forms with documentary poetics and the lyric essay. Like Leavitt and Ewing, Wadud calls our attention to the preconceived ideas we bring to the book as a cultural artifact, and the assumptions we make about language before it has even begun to unfold before us. *Crosslight forYoungbird* takes as one of its primary considerations the arbitrary categories we impose upon types of writing, distinctions that are actually more fluid than we tend to acknowledge. Wadud shows us that it is hybridity that creates a more complete account of shared experience, an artifact of cultural memory that is more just and more true.

Like Leavitt and Ewing, Wadud summons the reader's preconceived ideas about form and genre by attending to the work's appearance on the printed page. In "home 16 ways," for example, the pristine prose paragraphs create a semblance of order, and an artificial sense of unity, which the language itself interrogates and unravels. We encounter "a younbird" and its "able wings" alongside "bismillah calca" that "makes da bone firm." The reader is rendered suddenly and startlingly aware of the expectations they likely bring to prose—that the text will be consistent in the texture of its language, that it will be uniformly accessible and transparent in its meaning. Wadud provocatively writes against these readerly expectations of form and genre. Here, her audience is rendered, at turns, confidante and linguistic other, as the text is at certain moments suddenly inaccessible. By rendering us aware of the limitations that we impose upon prose, if only by looking at it on the page, Wadud ultimately works to foster more open-minded reading practices. For Wadud, seeing the limitations we place on language, and seeing the ways a containment of voice is gradually internalized, is the first step toward change. And change begins in language, as this is the very foundation of the social order.

She writes, for example, in "Calais, onward,"

> empire wrought boundless
> mollusked isle full of light
> moored light come light
> a sepulcher if not
> mark a journey supplicate
> pray mohammed
> and Fatima
> pray amira

Here Wadud creates a sense of "boundlessness" within the language of empire, ultimately working to expand what is possible within it. Like Leavitt and Ewing, Wadud uses the page as a visual field, creating a semblance of order and unity if only to call attention to their inherent artifice.

Wadud, Leavitt, and Ewing build on a Modernist inheritance of visual experimentation in poetry, ultimately using collage, hybridity, and performative language to challenge the limitations that readers impose upon their own voices. In doing so, these three gifted writers offer an expansive aesthetic, a poetics of inclusion and dialogue. By allowing many types of aesthetic experience and meaning-making to exist together in the same rhetorical space, they ultimately expand the boundaries of the book as a cultural artifact, allowing it to hold a shared history that is more just, more luminous, and more complete.

Exercises

1. Write a poem in which the visual elements tell part of the story.
2. Write a poem that sprawls outside of and beyond the boundaries of the printed page.
3. Write a poem that reads as an exercise in scale.

Works Cited

Ewing, Eve L. *Electric Arches*. Chicago: Haymarket Books, 2017.

Leavitt, Gracie. *Livingry*. New York: Nightboat Books, 2018.

Wadud, Asiya. *Crosslight for Youngbird*. New York: Nightboat Books, 2018.

A REVOLUTION IN POETIC LANGUAGE: HOW BOOKS CAN BUILD COMMUNITY

Kristina Marie Darling

For the past few decades, readers have witnessed a proliferation of small feminist presses run by women and nonbinary poets. These publishing projects, which include Leslie Scalapino's O Books, Lyn Hejinian's Tuumba Press, and Les Figues Press (edited by poets Teresa Carmody and Vanessa Place) have garnered an increasing amount of attention from literary scholars. Much of this critical work focuses on the role of women as cultural gatekeepers, particularly the ways that they have shaped, and offered provocative alternatives to, existing literary canons. This type of scholarship certainly remains vital and necessary. Yet feminist presses have also challenged prevailing ideas about the book as a cultural object, its limitations, and its possibilities.

Les Figues Press offers a unique glimpse into the ways feminist editors and publishers have renegotiated the boundaries of the printed book. Frequently pairing poetry with visual art, performance, and music, as well as other printed literary texts, the editors of Les Figues Press offer an expansive vision of what's possible within a poetry collection. The book as a cultural object becomes more inclusive. Perhaps more importantly, the editors of Les Figues Press have reimagined the relationship between the book and its audience. Rather than expecting the reader to passively accept meaning as given by the author, he or she is placed in a more active role. The reader is asked to forge connections between disparate voices, texts, and artistic mediums. What's more, the reader is asked to participate actively in the process of making meaning from the work. The editors, writers, and artists affiliated with Les Figues Press envision a more egalitarian relationship between artist and audience, in which the audience creates alongside the poet herself. The text appears in as many incarnations as there are readers. The work is never finished, but rather, is constantly in process.

In this essay, I discuss the innovative definition of the book that is set forth by the editors, writers, and artists at Les Figues Press. I examine the relationship between these books and the existing means of distribution, focusing on the ways in which this publisher has circumvented traditional ways of disseminating knowledge, thus creating alternative models. I argue that Les Figues Press not only challenges prevailing definitions of the book, but also reveals the channels of distribution as being predicated on the assumptions of a dominant literary culture. By offering an alternative definition of the book as cultural object, and the ways books can be distributed, Les Figues Press strives to democratize the book, an ideal that is largely made possible by twenty-first-century technology.

The Book as an Establishment: Renegotiating Boundaries

In their mission statement, the editors write, “In America, in this time, which is the early 21st century, we have inherited the clap of our fathers, i.e., applause sought and received for culture which is clotted.” This statement underscores many of the motivations behind starting a press like Les Figues. Contemporary female poets have been born into a long-standing literary tradition in which women’s texts are underrepresented. Perhaps more importantly, the existing means of dissemination make it difficult for these voices to gain inclusion in existing literary canons. In many ways, the editors’ description of culture as “clotted” suggests the difficulty of rendering cross-disciplinary feminist projects compatible with a system of distribution that operates on outmoded assumptions about the book, its limitations, and its possibilities.

For many editors working within feminist traditions, the book represents a mark of cultural legitimacy that has proven elusive for feminist artists working across artistic disciplines. These structures of cultural and institutional legitimating represent not only respect, but an economic sustainability that has remained inaccessible to many feminist writers who question the boundaries of existing genres, including the printed book. Les Figues Press presents a particularly striking example of how feminist editors, artists, and writers have strived to expand what's possible within the existing structures of cultural legitimacy. As Stephen Fredman explains, "The very need to invent, to attempt a new cultural grounding, has become one of the very hallmarks of poetry, which is always trying to explain to readers or find analogies to other cultural practices that will grant it legitimacy." Fredman's argument is useful for understanding the necessity, and even the inevitability, of these cultural markers of legitimacy within poetry. The editors at Les Figues Press have not chosen to accept these existing power structures, but rather, to work strategically within them, thus expanding what remains possible within culture.

This desire to make American print culture more inclusive remains especially visible in the editors' renegotiation of the boundaries of the printed book. The Les Figues Press catalogue includes what one might consider "traditional" manifestations of the printed book, which include anthologies (such as *I'll Drown My Book: Conceptual Writing by Women* and *The /N/Oulipian Analects*, a collection of essays about constraint-based writing) as well as translation projects. Yet these more conventional manifestations of the book are presented alongside collaborative, multidisciplinary, and participatory versions of the printed book.

Consider the Trench Art Series, in which three separate texts by individual writers are not only juxtaposed, but grouped together. The book becomes a collaborative endeavor, in which a writer's work is curated, then situated within a broader artistic conversation. One such pairing, the Trench Art maneuver series, presents Lily Hoang's *Aesthetic Statement*, *This is* by Teresa Carmody, and Harold Abramowitz's *Selected Writings*, and *Four Maneuvers* by the VD Collective, *I Statement* by Paul Hoover, and Matthew Timmons' *the old poetics*. These texts, unified by their authors' attempts to situate themselves within a literary landscape, together suggest the myriad forms that this type of engagement may take. By presenting creative work (such as Abramowitz's *Selected Writings*) alongside Timmons' more critical piece, as well as work that problematizes this distinction between "critical" and "creative" work, the editors ultimately complicate the texts they've published by grouping them in such a way. Indeed, this juxtaposition suggests that all writing, whether creative or overtly critical, is a theoretical act. Approached with these ideas in mind, the Trench Art series, in this case study and as a whole, presents a definition of the book as intertextual. The book is no longer presented in isolation, but rather, the editors underscore, for the reader, in the context of the artistic conversations in which the authors take part. The editors of Les Figues Press note that "The best-known trench art dates from World War I, when silversmiths in the trenches scavenged mortar shells and rifle bullets and warmed and wrought them into grand vases and radiant cruciform, as regular Smiths tapped out matchbook covers in scrap tin." Here aesthetic engagement arises in unlikely circumstances, from unlikely materials and unlikely individuals. In much the same way, the creation and dissemination of the book becomes an unlikely process of discovery, for writers, editors, and readers, all of whom are called upon to participate in the creation of the cultural knowledge associated with the book.

Such projects not only challenge the power structures associated with the printed book, but work within their confines to render the book more inclusive. One observes a similar impulse in the editors' forays into visual art and performance pieces associated with the printed book. More often than not, their events demand some form of participation on the part of the audience. An event, "Big City Forum: The Hub at WUHO," a literary reading featuring Allison Carter and Amina Cain, is described as "investigating liminal space and the articulation of experiences." In many ways, the event's structure forces the audience to articulate the experience of living between existing boundaries between forms and genres, as well as the ways in which art is experienced through the senses. Poems are heard, whereas visual art is seen, and in such an event, what one sees frequently complicates what one hears, and vice versa. This event, like many others, suggests that the most productive artistic spaces exist on the periphery of existing modes of communication, engagement, and dissemination.

In short, the work curated by Teresa Carmody and Vanessa Place presents an expansive definition of the book as cultural object. By doing so, the editors work to expand what remains possible within cultural exchanges, ultimately rendering the power structures associated with the book more inclusive for women, as well as for individuals whose project falls outside of established genre boundaries.

The Poet as Editor: Vanessa Place and Teresa Carmody

This concern with the boundaries between texts, discourses, and modes of dissemination remains one of the most pressing concerns of both editors' own creative work. For both Carmody and Place, the poet's task is to question, challenge, and problematize the power structures reflected in these demarcations. The press itself affords a place for dialogue, in which the editors can explore this same problem in ways that are not possible for a poet working on a single-author project. The press becomes a unique collaborative space, a source of discovery and possibility for both author and editor.

Vanessa Place, for example, has frequently explored the connection between appropriation and critical thinking, suggesting that the idea of "ownership" of a text reflects larger power structures within society and the academy. In many ways, Place challenges the idea that texts retain discrete boundaries, that one individual's ideas can be neatly separated from those of a collective. She writes in an interview for *Bomb* that

> This shifts the locus of the work to its recipient, necessarily embodied, necessarily affected. What is boredom, after all, if not maximal minimal affect? The question of materiality is closer here to a medieval notion of materialism in which the highest form of materiality is that which is transformed by nothing but the divino spiritu—such as the Eucharist. These categories are no longer so discrete as each becomes not inherent in the stuff, but one of its categorical imperatives.

In this discussion of conceptual writing, Place questions the distinction between artist and audience, suggesting that the reader retains a crucial role in creating meaning from a given text. Just as "the locus of the work" is "shifted" to the reader, Place ultimately problematizes the idea that the author retains ownership over a given work. Indeed, this idea that the boundaries of a work remain porous and permeable seems to be one of the unifying ideas behind Place's curatorial decisions.

Teresa Carmody's work, too, reflects a concern with the ownership of literary texts, and a desire to render the boundaries of a given poem more permeable. Her book *Eye Hole Adore* explores relationships, which seem at first to be personal but quickly introduce questions of literary, cultural, and artistic legacy. She writes in an untitled prose piece,

> Sometimes she became sullen, and I tried everything to make her stop, frivolous, sullen, moping, angry, affected, dishearten'd, atheist. I'd massage her, accuse her, blame her, kiss her. I'd yell and tell her what to do, beg, please please, cheer up. Change the attitude, that's all. Here, let me listen. If it was Friday, I'd make her favorite red beans with Bhutanese red rice and red velvet cake, and if it was Wednesday, I'd make her blue potatoes with rosemary, blue corn muffins and spicy chokeberry sauce. Thursdays were easiest: pink lemonade with Mother's iced animal cookies.

Here the speaker's voice is revealed as socially constructed. The voice is no longer singular, but rather, is permeated by history, culture, and the discourses to which one has been subjected. As in Place's work, Carmody questions the idea of ownership of a literary text, suggesting that all work is collaborative in nature, and authorship never takes place in isolation. When considered in light of her editorial work, Carmody's poetry reflects a similar concern with the boundaries between texts, mediums, and modes of dissemination. Indeed, both Carmody and Place call upon the reader to recognize the porous and permeable boundaries between literary/artistic texts, and to account for them in the ways that literary works are disseminated to readers.

Redefining the Function of the Book: The Poetic Text as Fascinating Community

The editors' renegotiation of the boundaries of the book as a cultural object also implies a reenvisioning of the function of the book. For the editors, writers, and artists associated with Les Figues

Press, the book is not a static object, but rather a forum for dialogue and exchange between members of a given artistic community. The book, its parameters, its meaning, and its participants remain constantly in flux.

This impulse remains especially visible in the press's performance projects, which are frequently organized to promote new titles. Consider the book launch for *I'll Drown My Book: Conceptual Writing by Women*. The editors describe the event as requiring "some assembly" on the part of the audience, as authors included in the anthology are "distributed" across the city at three alternative venues, allowing readers to choose the order in which they experience the work. Just as the anthology itself offers an alternative canon of women's writing, which problematizes and supplements existing bodies of work, the book launch allows the reader to participate in shaping the canon. The spectator may choose to omit, include, and reorder the writers selected for inclusion. The book launch effectively democratizes the process of constructing a literary canon. Approached with these ideas in mind, the book itself serves as merely an occasion for this conversation about power and authority within the literary community and in the academy.

Along these lines, Les Figues Press's Not Content series, a "year-long series of text projects" curated by the editors, challenges the audience to participate actively in the creation of the text itself. The project problematizes the idea that a book is a static object with a single fixed meaning. For the editors, these assumptions about the book ultimately foreclose the possibility of creating and fostering literary community. Projects like Not Content serve not only as a corrective to previous models of the relationship between reader and text, but they also open new possibilities for conceiving of the book in a changing literary and artistic landscape. Consider the "Explanation as Composition" audio opening, which included such participants as Kate Durbin, Aimee Bender, Allison Carter, Mark

Z. Danielewski, Janice Lee, Harryette Mullen, Janet Sarbanes, Anna Joy Springer, and Stephen Van Dyck. The project offers "six narrative experiences," from which participants can choose "story," "geography," "ekphrasis," "provenance," "nature," or "confession." This gesture suggests the difficulty of extricating writer and reader, artist and audience, book and consumer. The text itself is shaped by the expectations of an audience, whether it anticipates, conforms to, or problematizes them. The boundaries of a literary text, then, are constantly being negotiated and renegotiated. A text is never a static object with a single fixed meaning, but rather, offers a proliferation of meaning. This impulse also remains visible in the Trench Art series, in which the text becomes an occasion for recognizing oneself as part of an existing artistic conversation.

For the editors of Les Figues Press, this multiplicity of meanings, participants, and possibilities within a literary text is not a novel concept. Rather, voice has always been a social construct, and the means of cultural production and dissemination should account for this. Their innovative definition of the book, then, calls for a renegotiation of the ways books are distributed to readers.

Les Figues Press and the Channels of Distribution

More often than not, such an innovative definition of the book cannot be accommodated by the established channels of distribution. The existing modes of dissemination are frequently predicated on the assumption that the book is a static entity, with a single fixed meaning. As Edward Mack argues, these "modes of book production, promotion, and consumption shape ideas of literary value." The text that cannot be disseminated, then, becomes the "illegitimate" text, a work that has been deprived of value within the academy. Les Figues Press strives to expand what is possible within the existing modes of dissemination, allowing more texts, and a greater diversity of voices, to gain recognition within the existing structures of cultural production. In doing so, they frequently turn to alternative modes of dissemination, challenging readers, writers, and cultural producers to expand their definition of what it means for a text to be distributed, and, as a result, legitimized.

Consider the use of grassroots fundraising to finance the printing of *I'll Drown My Book: Conceptual Writing by Women*. By utilizing Kickstarter, a platform that allows individuals and organizations to donate to a cause, releasing the funds once the project has met its target amount, the press was able to circumvent traditional fundraising procedures. Rather than submitting proposals to state, local, and national arts agencies, which may not recognize the expansive definition of the book promulgated by Les Figues Press, the editors were able to mobilize individuals who wanted to see change within the academy and a revision of the power structures dictating canon formation and cultural production. In their project statement for Kickstarter, for instance, the editors write that "Conceptual writing is emerging as a vital 21st-century literary movement and Les Figues Press wants to represent the contributions of women in this defining moment. By supporting this project, you will ensure that women claim their literary space." The editors of Les Figues Press clearly see their editorial undertaking, as well as the means of disseminating the work, as a corrective action. What proves most noteworthy about this intervention is that the editors do not simply seek legitimacy for texts, but rather they seek to expand our definition of legitimacy by offering alternative models of gatekeeping practices, cultural production, and dissemination. Their expansive notion of what constitutes a book is merely one facet of this larger project.

With that said, the Kickstarter campaign also underscores the centrality of web-based technology to this type of cultural intervention. Consider Les Figues Press's use of social media sites like Facebook to connect with readers. The editors frequently use these technologies to mobilize grassroots support in much the same way as they did with the Kickstarter campaign. Approached with these ideas in mind, Les Figues Press offers a critique of a limiting definition of the book, as well as the power structures that dictate who defines the book. By reaching out to the public, rather than existing cultural authorities, for support, Les Figues Press calls for a democratization of the process of cultural production. The following comment was posted to the press's Facebook page: "Did you miss the Les Figues auction? We're having an excess, extra online-only auction this weekend only. Work by Check it out." Here one observes a concerted effort to mobilize readers who desire change in the form of alternative models of production, dissemination, and consumption. Web-based technologies serve to democratize who can participate in these processes, ultimately affording the possibility of revising the power structures inherent in the production of literary texts.

Moreover, these alternative models of fundraising, cultural production, and disseminating literary texts accommodate projects that may not fit within existing definitions of the book. The items promoted through such sites as Facebook, Myspace, Twitter/X, Blogspot, etc., frequently include multimedia text-based projects, art objects, and other items that fall outside the traditional definition of "book." Divya Victor's Hellocasts offers one especially striking example. Her project, a retranscription of Charles Reznikov's book *Holocaust*, is described as a "poetic composition that appropriates the transcriptions from the speech of witnesses at the Eichmann and Nuremberg trials—into the shape of Hello Kitty." Taking the form of an installation of text, which spectators literally inhabit, Victor's project uses this format to explore notions of voicelessness, silence(ing), and personal responsibility. She writes in her artist statement,

> Hello Kitty, the cat, has no mouth. Hello Kitty, the brand, always speaks for itself; is always spoken for by its consumer; is a felicific felicitation of affirmed desires. The brand is the document of a figure's reluctance to speak for itself. What is the distinction between the event of the Holocaust and the documents that brand it?

The form of the installation ultimately allows for an overwhelming sensory experience of the text, something that proves less possible with a book as traditionally imagined. Just as the project itself asks us to reexamine our definition of the book, the editors' treatment of the finished product challenges us to reconsider what it means for a text to be distributed to audiences. Does the fact that a viewer has experienced a text mean that it has been disseminated? Can cultural gatekeeping manifest itself, and be documented, in new ways, which may or may not encompass a permanent artifact such as a book? These questions, posed by Victor and the editors promoting her work, suggest that the answers are constantly changing. Approached with these ideas in mind, their efforts not only expand our definition of the book as a cultural object, but they suggest ways in which the channels of distribution may become more inclusive, and accommodate alternative definitions of the book.

Technology and the Printed Book: Democratizing the Poetic Text

The editors at Les Figues Press strive for a democratization of the poetic text. Not only does the book become an occasion for dialogue, but the definition of a book, its boundaries, its limitations, and its possibilities, remain constantly in flux. As Nicky Marsh argues in *Democracy in Contemporary Women's Poetry*, the existing definition of the book remains predicated on a model of publishing that "valorizes the individual." Presses like Les Figues reveal these assumptions as being outmoded, particularly when considering the possibilities for collaboration afforded by new technologies.

Much of the conceptual writing published by Les Figues Press exemplifies this notion of the book as being a collaborative endeavor, one that is made possible largely by new technologies. Consider Matthew Timmons' work in *The New Poetics*, a title available from Les Figues Press's Trench Art Series. Like many of the books published by Les Figues, Timmons' work offers readers a poetics of appropriation, in which found language is situated in a new context, thus prompting the reader to become more conscious of the historicity of language. He writes in a piece entitled "The New Emotion,"

> The New Emotion is a collection of movement; Automatic Mechanical Self-Winding Movement. The key concept of The New Emotion is a multimodal presentation by a lifelike agent of emotion expression. The computing industry of the 1980s enabled significantly higher image quality, boosting diagnostic accuracy with less radiation exposure, giving us The New Emotion. Both formats were sanctioned by the child-rearing theories of the day in which the father was admired for displaying The New Emotion while still remaining a function of The New Emotions.

Here Timmons questions conventional notions of authorship, particularly the purported "ownership" of literary texts. He gestures at the ways in which new technologies have rendered the idea of authorship a problematic, if not impossible, concept. For the editors of Les Figues Press, too, any text is a collaboration, even more so in today's technological and cultural landscape.

Rather than attempting to resurrect this outmoded literary ideal, Place and Carmody embrace the increasingly collaborative nature of the poetic text, and seek to further democratize the creation, dissemination, and analysis of poetry. More often than not, the editors have promoted work that encourages the reader to participate actively in creating meaning from the text. The reader simultaneously inhabits the roles of artist, critic, and participant, ultimately problematizing that one retains a single fixed relationship to a given book or literary text. Consider Les Figues Press's Trench Art Series. By pairing multiple texts, and suggesting some discernible relationship between the authors' work, the editors encourage the reader to articulate the connection between these literary texts, and to describe (whether to oneself or one's artistic community) the conversation taking place between writers selected for inclusion. The book becomes a collaboration between writers, but also between artist and audience. It is the audience, and their participation, which actualizes the meaning of the work, the significance of the conversation taking place in each Trench Art set.

Often the editors turn to emerging web-based technologies to accommodate this notion of the collaborative text. Just as collaborations are made possible by search engines, the web, and the general availability of information as a result of these technologies, these resources have also made possible the dissemination of these increasingly collaborative texts. For example, the editors use a central website to reinforce the connection between various authors' work in the Trench Art Series. While major online retailers (such as Amazon.com, BarnesandNoble.com, and Alibris.com) are predicated on a single-author model of the book as a cultural institution, the relative ease of creating and promoting websites democratizes not only the poetic text, but also the ability to define its boundaries.

Indeed, Les Figues Press reinscribes the boundaries of the book as a cultural object, and this gesture remains especially apparent in the organization of their website. The category of the book is made to encompass not only the text itself, but also its wider context (in terms of the writerly conversation to which it belongs), and its process. The fact that the site includes a "cahiers" series, or "notebooks," within the category of the book, suggests that a book is always in process. Whether the writer revises, revisits, and repurposes the text, or its meaning is constantly inscribed and reinscribed by readers, the book ceases to be a static object, but rather, is always in flux.

In this regard, the fact that Les Figues Press utilizes social media technologies to reach out to a public readership suggests the centrality of the reader in actualizing the book. In their mission statement, the editors describe Les Figues as "creating aesthetic conversations," and, to a great extent, this ideal is made possible by technology. The democratization of the means of production and dissemination allows greater agency for the individual in defining the book, its boundaries, and its possibilities. As a result, readers may choose not only the communities in which they participate, but they may call for change within those communities, and within the culture at large. Indeed, these emergent technologies have allowed a renegotiation of the book as a cultural object, as well as its production, dissemination, and its participants. This approach authorizes the reader as a crucial part of the work, and the work is made increasingly available to readers through novel channels of distribution. As a result, our notion of what constitutes dissemination for a literary work is not only problematized, but rendered more inclusive, reflecting a shifting literary and technological landscape.

Conclusion

Les Figues Press offers an alternative definition of the book as a cultural object, as well as what it means for a text to be disseminated to readers. By doing so, the editors at Les Figues strive to expand what is possible within the existing structures of cultural production. They work strategically within existing modes of cultural production, not only problematizing them, but working to render them more inclusive. Their vision of the book, rather than valorizing the individual author, is markedly collaborative, allowing for a democratization of the book and its participants.

Place and Carmody, through their curatorial efforts, reveal the book as a cultural institution predicated on outmoded assumptions about authorship, and about the ownership of literary texts. Because the available channels of distribution for books are predicated on these beliefs, texts that fall outside of this definition of the book become difficult to disseminate, and thus to gain legitimacy in the eyes of cultural authorities. A text that cannot be disseminated becomes a nonentity, an "illegitimate text." The editors at Les Figues Press strive for an expansive definition of the book, but also for what it means for a text to be distributed. Does the fact that a text has reached an appreciative audience mean that it has been disseminated? Do the channels of distribution limit what is possible within the book as a literary form? The editors do not pose clear-cut answers to these questions, but rather, ask us to become conscious of these issues, and to begin a conversation about them.

The editorial decisions of Les Figues Press posit the book as an occasion for dialogue. The book is no longer a static object, but rather, it remains constantly in flux as its borders, participants, and meaning are constantly being renegotiated. This impulse toward conceiving of the book as being in process remains especially apparent in the grouping of literary texts in the Trench Art Series, as well as in the editors' concerted efforts (particularly in curating events such as book launches and installations) to present the book as an ongoing project, which readers help to actualize. The book is no longer something over which the author takes ownership, but rather, something that remains inherently democratic in terms of its participation, meaning, and dissemination.

Much of this critique of the book as a cultural institution is made possible by emergent web-based technologies. Social networking sites, as well as alternative fundraising models like Kickstarter, allow the editors not only to bypass the traditional means of dissemination, but to challenge conventional ideas about what it means for a text to be disseminated. Indeed, these efforts suggest that cultural gatekeeping mechanisms may manifest themselves in ways that have not been heretofore considered. In other words, the fact that readers have mobilized around an alternative definition of the book, as evidenced by participation in events, aesthetic conversations, and the texts themselves, suggests that individuals do retain a certain degree of agency when deciding which cultural texts are worthwhile endeavors. Les Figues Press, in many ways, seeks to democratize the book not only by proffering alternative models of what a book should be, but also by asking how cultural institutions like the book are defined, regulated, and maintained. Place and Carmody gesture toward the possibility of harnessing existing channels of distribution, while at the same time rendering them more inclusive.

Discussion Questions

1. What is the relationship between language and power? What is the relationship between publishing and power?
2. How do we interact differently with published vs. unpublished works, or books disseminated in an untraditional format?
3. Where do these ideas about textual legitimacy come from? When did you first encounter them?

Works Cited

Carmody, Teresa. *Eye Hole Adore*. PS Books, 2008.

Fredman, Stephen. *The Grounding of American Poetry*. Cambridge: Cambridge University Press, 2009.

Mack, Edward. *Manufacturing Modern Japanese Literature*. Durham, NC: Duke University Press, 2010.

Marsh, Nicky. *Democracy in Contemporary Women's Poetry*. London: Palgrave MacMillan, 2007.

Place, Vanessa. Interview, "Poetry and the Conceptualist Period." *Bomb*, March 5, 2012. https://bombmagazine.org/articles/2012/03/05/vanessa-place-poetry-and-the-conceptualist-period/.

Victor, Divya, and Vanessa Place. *Hellocasts by Charles Reznikoff*. Ood Press, 2010.

PART THREE

Understanding the Constructed Nature of Community

NEGOTIATING THE PROBLEM OF COMMUNITY AS A WRITER OF COLOR

Wendy Chen

Writing can often feel like a solitary and individual practice. As a writer, you might spend hours alone at a desk working on a piece of writing that will never be shown to anyone else. And yet, I find that every time I sit down to write by myself, the conversations I have had with others in my community are what keep me writing. Finding and building a community for yourself can not only create lasting relationships and friendships, but also become a critical part of your writing practice. After all, a writing community can help you develop and hone your own voice, become a more generous reader for yourself and others, and offer intellectual challenge and inspiration.

However, while there are many ways to find and build community, the idea of community itself can be a fraught and complicated notion. In my own experience as a Chinese American woman, an understanding of what community is often comes out of an understanding of and encounter with what community isn't—namely, a sense of exclusion and diminishment. Thus, for writers of color in America, the journey toward a supportive and nurturing community can be arduous and ever-evolving—one that might never be reached but rather always strived for. Indeed, for writers of color, a supportive community may never be able to exist without simultaneously being a site of uneasy tensions, negotiations, and encounters.

How can writers of color navigate their way toward a fulfilling community? What characterizes collaborative and communal spaces that may feel more welcoming to writers of color? What characterizes spaces that may feel hostile to writers of color? How can we as writers of color foster sustainable spaces of collaboration and community for ourselves?

To address some of these concerns, I want to begin from a place of my own experiences—of particularities rather than generalities. Every writer of color has a different, complex relationship with the idea of community; by no means do I wish to present my experiences as representative of all. However, in conversations with other writers of color, I have come to realize that aspects of my experiences with the question of community are not just unique to me. Ultimately, I hope my experiences can provide not only affirmation for those who may have negotiated similar experiences around the idea of community, but also serve as an entryway into the larger conversation of building community for writers of color.

I first experienced a sense of community as a writer through encounters with my earliest mentors. In elementary school, my teachers greatly supported my interest in writing, and their encouragement was invaluable to my development as a writer. The more I expressed interest, the more my teachers introduced me to different books to read. The more I read, however, the more I realized that the authors of the books from the school library and the ones we studied in class—including visiting writers—were not like me at all. Moreover, the subject matter and characters they wrote about were also not like me. Indeed, for the most part, my exposure to writers or subject matter that represented someone like myself would have occurred during what was then termed Asian-Pacific American Heritage Month. Over the years, this awareness solidified into a sense of alienation. Writers who looked like me were not part of the larger writing community; if we did appear, we would be relegated to a well-defined and limited space and time.

Thus, my early exposure to encouragement and support was complicated by this growing awareness of alienation. Of course, the complexity of this experience is not just limited to my development as a writer, but rather is a part of growing up in America as a woman of color. When I look back at my early childhood writings, I notice a point at which the main characters in my stories are no longer Chinese or Chinese American but rather white. Even as a child, I realized—without anyone explicitly teaching me—that the stories I wanted to tell were not stories that interested the writing community I had learned about in the classroom.

This speaks, I believe, to the importance of how we represent the writing community through teaching and mentorship. So often, within the institution of academia, community becomes institutionalized as well. Thus, the syllabus—which represents for students the site where writers are brought together as an intellectual community within the classroom—becomes institutionalized as canon; canon then is viewed as an always-was and always-will-be community of writers who are "worthy" to learn from and study—indeed, historical mentors.

There have been efforts, of course, to change the way the writing community is represented inside the classroom. Pushback against change, however, can be vigorous. Criticism of the canon is, after all, a criticism of community, which feels personal.

While I am using the idea of community within academic spaces as an example, I am not just speaking to the space within academia. Just as there are those who are attached to an idea of the canon within the classroom, so too there are those who are attached to the way the writing community has been predominantly historically represented outside the classroom.

When communities become institutionalized, we think of them as sites we enter rather than ones we create. These sites might appear as if they have always existed, indeed as cultural pillars. Nevertheless, it is imperative to question how and for what purpose these communities were made. What was or is the aim of these communities? Who is a part of these communities in this current moment? Who is not a part of these communities? Who gets to decide?

By examining how these and other communities are constructed and, consequently, by placing emphasis on the constructed nature of these communities, we are also emphasizing the building of community as a process. By providing greater transparency behind the construction of communities or even modeling community building in action, teachers and mentors can pass along the skills to build new communities.

After all, the communities that serve us as writers today will not necessarily be the ones that serve writers in the future. This ephemeral nature of our communities is not a quality to mourn but rather one to embrace and encourage.

Indeed, one of the most valuable lessons I have learned from being within communities is understanding how to organize, collaborate, and build communities with others. Witnessing how communities have resolved—or failed to resolve—conflict and succeeded in establishing themselves—or failed in their projects—has been invaluable to me in my own endeavors to build communities. For writers of color for whom existing communities may not fully serve, being in communities that empower them to build their own can be impactful far into the future.

Finding or building communities that represent who you are can drastically change the way you see your work. Supportive communities for writers of color can provide a stable space within which to have difficult conversations that might otherwise be met with hostility. Mentors and friends of color have provided indispensable advice for how to navigate a predominantly white publishing world. They have helped guide me through questions that have no easy answers, or no answers at all. For example, are these white editor's criticisms something to consider, or are they asking me to compromise myself in ways I should resist? Am I myself making compromises in my own writing for a white audience? How do I write about pain as a person of color without making that pain a spectacle for a white audience?

The mentors and friends I have made in the communities I have been a part of have helped me through times of paralyzing self-doubt. Often, listening to other writers of color offer up their own experiences with negotiating these difficult questions can clarify the kinds of choices I want to make in my own work. Knowing that others have felt the same way as I have makes sitting down to write that much easier.

Communities of color can provide resources of mentorship, friendship, knowledge, and opportunities that writers of color might not as readily encounter or access outside of these spaces. I have noticed that the communities of color I have been a part of often rely heavily on oral history or word of mouth to convey sensitive information. Sometimes this is out of fear of reprisals from influential white figures in the larger writing world. Sometimes this is due to the difficulty of writing down distressing experiences. There are certainly many other reasons for what I have observed. By no means am I suggesting that communities of color are the only spaces within which to have these kinds of conversations—only that communities in which writers of color feel comfortable expressing themselves are likely to encourage these dialogues.

The dialogue and conversations I have had or encountered with other writers of color have not only fundamentally changed the way I see my work, but also the way I see myself as a writer and woman of color. I cannot imagine being the writer or person I am today without all the mentors and friends I have had the luck to encounter within these spaces of community.

Frequently, these relationships have lasted even when the

particular community within which they formed has not. Moreover, many of these relationships have ended up being the basis for the formation of new communities. New communities like email chains, workshops, literary magazines, and more might never have been formed without the failure of countless other communities.

No community is perfect, after all—no matter how much they might try to be. More and more, there are communities that describe themselves as safe spaces for people of color. These communities may fail at their aims even with the best of intentions. Communities that appear welcoming at first are sometimes hostile upon entrance. I have observed such communities objectify and showcase their members of color as proof of their diversity, as well as ostracize members of color for being "troublemakers" when they suggest change. I have heard community leaders accuse members of color of ingratitude for their admittance into the community in the first place. In these moments, I did not feel grateful at all to be a part of these communities.

To a certain extent, this is, perhaps, to be expected. Some spaces can certainly feel safer than others for people of color, but can truly safe spaces ever exist within the framework of a racist society? This is not to suggest that we should stop trying to create safe spaces for people of color. Failure can be traumatic, violent, and aggressive. Failure can also, however, be productive and generative—and push us toward new dialogues we might not otherwise have had. Indeed, I have observed that community leaders who view their communities and themselves as infallible often react the strongest against criticism. Every criticism of their communities is seen as an accusation of racism—a personal attack. When viewed in this light, the term "racist" itself becomes monstrous, even taboo.

However, I wonder if, just as we have reconsidered our relationship to failure, we can reconsider our relationship to the term "racist." Instead of starting from the point of view that no one is racist, perhaps we can start from the point of view that everyone is. This is not a personal attack but rather an observation of the biases we absorb from a racist society. As Ibram X. Kendi writes in *How to Be an Antiracist*:

> It happens for me in successive steps, these steps to be an antiracist.
> I stop using the "I'm not a racist" or "I can't be racist" defense of denial.
> I admit to the definition of racist (someone who is supporting racist policies or expressing racist ideas).
> I confess the racist policies I support and racist ideas I express.
> I accept their source (my upbringing inside a nation making us racist). (226)

If we begin from a less defensive stance, criticisms or calls for change no longer appear as inflammatory attacks against the character of the community, but as genuine efforts to change that community for the better. A less defensive stance can, ultimately, facilitate more introspection and dialogue.

After all, a community is a Platonic ideal toward which we are always building, but may never reach. Therefore, community itself is a process. Communities are not static but rather ever-evolving—breaking apart, then coming back together in new and previously unimaginable forms. In the space of communities, diversity should not be a prize to be won but rather part of a process of creation, collaboration, and evolution.

For writers of color, community can be a difficult idea to negotiate. It has been for me. I am not the first writer of color to struggle with the question of community, nor will I be the last. Writers of color must frequently bear the burden of finding or carving out their own communities and spaces, not to mention acquiring the skills to do so. Furthermore, some of my most alienating experiences have occurred within the structure of communities. As a writer of color, negotiating your way toward community can be a challenging and frustrating journey that never ends. However, at their best, communities can offer writers of color transformative approaches to collaboration and encounter.

Writing Exercises

1. Think of a community of which you are a member. What is the history of that community? Does an official version of the history already exist? Write your own version of that history that reflects the values you treasure most about your community.

2. How have the histories of your communities been passed down—if they have at all? Are they passed down through the written word, oral storytelling, or some other form of communication? Who has gotten to tell these histories? Who has been left out of these histories? Write a narrative examining the history of these community histories.

3. What are some new communities that can or will emerge from your existing communities? Write a proposal for one of them.

4. Have communities changed the way you see yourself as a writer? Write a reflection explaining why or why not.

5. What skills have you learned from being within your communities? Write a reflection detailing how you can apply them toward building communities of your own.

Works Cited

Kendi, Ibram X. *How to Be an Antiracist*. New York: One World, 2019.

CONNECTION ACROSS LINES OF DIFFERENCE: TEACHING TO BUILD COMMUNITY AND FOSTER SOCIAL CHANGE

Ming Holden

My second day at work in Kenya, I found myself standing in front of a group of refugee sex workers in Nairobi, asked with a half-hour's notice to do some kind of creative writing exercise with them.

I folded and refolded my hands in front of me in my blue jeans, hand-me-down shirt, and the Airwalk sneakers I got for $8 at JC Penny in Indiana. The women, all refugees engaged in "survival sex," sat in chairs in a stuffy room near the poor neighborhood of Eastleigh, where a great deal of Nairobi's refugees settle. They were somewhere between the ages of 13 and 50. One had a baby with her. They all looked at me, some with welcoming smiles, some with guarded expressions.

I couldn't blame the latter. I was what's called an "operational partner" of the refugee agencies sponsoring the workshop—the United Nations High Commissioner for Refugees (UNHCR) and the German organization GTZ—but not a staff member. I had no badge. Any time I wanted a ride to visit one of the women I worked with, I had to wait in the quiet, leafy interior of the UNHCR compound for one of the six Community Services staff members to have a free couple of hours, since the vehicle was not allowed to move with me as the only passenger and the lumbering convoy, a white beast with a large radio antenna affixed to the hood like a rhino horn, got nowhere fast. I didn't speak French or Swahili; outside of four months of a part-time job working with at-risk high schoolers, I am not trained as a social worker; and I was on the kind of budget that requires editing documents for other *mzungus* (white folks) in order to afford my stay in Kenya.

I was not on the kind of budget that forced me to do sex work in Nairobi slums, however, and as James—the Community Services director at UNHCR whose gentle presence and clean black suit attracted the respectful attention of the women—introduced me in a language I couldn't understand, I studied the wall behind him: columns of markered signs in English reading "Decision-Making," "Safe Sex Practice," "Coping with Stress." I looked out at the moist faces, and felt like I did years ago in Ecuador as I observed a gentle, calm *doctora* at a family-planning practice, speaking with a teenage mother of three children who wept through a black eye with fear that her husband would find out she'd asked about birth control. In some sort of voyeur's Tourette's, I couldn't stop from imagining her being beaten, or a shadowy figure mounting her against her will.

* * *

Standing in front of the room I cast about internally for some bridge to the women engaged in survival sex, human beings whose pasts were such horrors and whose trauma was not over. What could I say to them, in 10 minutes, through a translator, about creative writing that would help victims of some of humanity's worst atrocities?

Seasoned peace-and-justice workers will tell you two things: one, that bringing a relatively untrained young professional into a room full of past and current trauma victims with little warning runs many risks, including that of retraumatizing them; and two, that it does not help anyone to minimize one's own suffering. I hadn't heard either of those things yet, and the workshop coordinator, Monica, stood beside me at the front of the room, ready to translate. I began to speak with no command of the room and while I did not cower, I spoke more meekly than I wanted to, pausing for Monica to relate my messages.

"First I would like to say it is an honor to be here and to be with you. I want you to know that there are many women besides me who, even across the world, think of you, think of what women go through here. We feel you. We hear you and we see you."

There were some kind nods among the older women. One of the women was curvy with short hair, and her neighbor kept an arm around her neck. I started thinking of the strongest, wisest people I knew. What had they told me, in dark times? I had over the past year recovered from what various doctors called "post-traumatic stress disorder," "damaged neurotransmitters," "learned helplessness." I had learned things about the nervous system and the brain and how trauma affects the body and mind, and how that effect corresponds to the thoughts we have. My experience with trauma was a real one, and recovery from it a bundle of lessons I wanted badly to share, but a million variables kept me from knowing if it would help: would it translate, technically, emotionally, culturally? Would any of it help when trauma continued to batter the experience of these women, and when what they saw and underwent as part of their plight and flight as refugees was as horrific, as unspeakable, as it was? I couldn't help but compare; their trauma was worse.

Some of the women were dressed in pants and texting on their cell phones; some were in brightly patterned wrap dresses. Their face shapes and tones varied, blossoms in a meadow. In my mind, I heard them: my mentor Stacey saying *we need to bear witness to each other's lives*. My aunt standing at her sink, saying, *you can train your thoughts, it really is possible*. My martial arts sensei, whose PTSD from

Vietnam lasted decades: *Your spirit and heart are fine, it's just the mind. The mind is like a computer. You can always press restart.* My cousin Darcy, again and again: *You create your own reality. Thoughts and words have power and energy.* A friend of mine in social work describing dealing with trauma as being "in the trauma space."

I looked down at my sneakers, over at Monica, around at the women. "I thought I would share one or two things that helped me cope with stress," I said to them, pausing for Monica to translate. "One of the things that has helped me through the times of feeling terrible and ashamed is to stop feeling like those things were *inside* me. Instead I started thinking of painful terrible feelings like a space I was in, a room." A few of the women were nodding.

"Then the terrible feeling isn't me, it's only a room I spend time in sometimes. Sometimes we're in the room a long time." I thought back to nearly a year ago, when I began graduate school: humid heat, sweating into our chairs during orientation week with a pedagogy director above whose head I kept seeing flicks and specks. I was afraid my peers could sense somehow the muscle flutters and cramps that peppered my body. I thought about the mediocre words I had written in the margins of my notebook that week describing it: *a feeble creekbed creature, black-slimed, dry-lunged.*

"One of the most important parts of creative writing, of poetry, is simile or metaphor—saying a thing is another thing, like that a baby is a beautiful moon," I said. "I wonder if you have any examples for how it feels to be in the dark room. I sometimes feel like a river creature, a fish, in a dry riverbed, moving slowly in the sun with no water to nourish me. Do you have any other pictures in your mind for that feeling, for that room?"

Monica translated the question and then, when a few hands came up, their answers.

"Like I am drowning," said one slender woman.

"Like the house has burned down and it is only me standing," said another, fanning herself with her notebook.

But *was* that a metaphor? *Had* her house burned down? I looked at this young woman, whose face was shaped like a heart and whose expression told me she was not convinced. In that moment, neither was I, but I nodded at each of the answers, maintaining eye contact with the speaker, and kept on.

"Thank you for those examples. The next part of the exercise is a metaphor for how it feels when we are at our best and feeling happy." My example came from the Annie Dillard quote: "*The impulse to save something good for a better place later is a signal to spend it now. Something more will arise for later, something better. These things fill from behind, from beneath, like well water.*"

"I feel like I am a well," I said, "and I fill with good things from beneath, things that nourish what is around me like water feeds grass and trees. What do you feel like?"

"Like I am a tree."

"Like I am hugging my family."

"Like I am seeing my husband again after a long time apart, like I am seeing my children."

Once again the line of metaphor blurred. Back in college, we discussed a poem someone suggested as an elegy for a dead friend in a poetry workshop years ago, a poem that would not be words but a marble-inked page, and the poem by Neruda himself an exile—with the lines, "in the streets the blood of the children / ran simply, like the blood of children." There are no similes for the worst loss, no metaphors for the most horrific experiences, the argument went. What could I say?

* * *

The question of what to say to the sex workers in Eastleigh about creative writing could be put another way: what does literature serve to *do*? *Whom* does it serve? The half-circle of women in my mind, who would go home that evening to God knows what, breathed new life into the old question. I looked around at the faces, wondering. The wealthy scion who wonders if there is a point to life, the street child who wonders if there is any way out: can words help anyone can stories help *anyone*, regardless of their situation? Can literature be company for the lonely, solace for the crowded, a remove for the stressed and a return for the removed? Words have stirred people to action, to mutiny; they have done the opposite and cleansed the hearts of the aching in catharsis. What are the limits, if limits there are, to what it can do and whom it can help . . . if a society is war-torn, if a person is scarred by trauma, how does that change the role of words—in a free society, in a prison?

What is the *function* of literature? How and when does that function change? In a warring society, in a censored society, in a free society? How could it function for these women?

"I know this may seem very ineffective and small to do," I said to them. It was afternoon in East Africa; when it's not bucketing rain that bathes the flame tree blossoms a brighter orange, it is dusty and sweltering. The women shifted in their seats. We went back and forth, Odette with the heart-shaped face the vociferous doubter of words I could see the argument against.

"Odette says there is no way to get around the terrible memories she has."

James stepped out for a cup of tea, and the room only had girls in it now. It was what I needed.

Up came the memory of standing with my back to the camera in New York, in an artist's suite on 8th Avenue near Penn Station. I had figure modeled in college and reasoned to myself that a friendly girl behind the camera obviated the tone of the man doing the Calvin Klein-style voice-over as he suggested I pull my pants down to just under the butt cheek, and I did, for $100 cash. Broke because I didn't feel safe among the various mental and substance abuses at home. Because I couldn't find work due to the fact that my primary professional reference was the same person who had behaved in ways mentors, in a perfect world, would not—ways that would ultimately lead to stress hormones inundating my system so often for so long that my nervous system started firing as though I'd just stepped on a mine all day long. Up came the memory of after a boy I loved had told me I was the girl-before-the-new-girlfriend: the sexually transmitted infection HPV showed up on my female exam. For four months, five years ago, but it was there, and the shame consumed my body with electric bouts of pain.

And up came the memory of my sinking feeling at the knock on the door, the one that stopped the Planned Parenthood doctor in latex gloves from inserting my IUD. There was only one reason a nurse would knock on that door at that moment. I was standing in a conference room in Nairobi, and somehow also I was writhing and moaning, spitting over the side of the gurney, sweating and shivering by turns in shock as they vacuumed out what I called my sea monkey and carried it out in a dixie cup.

Odette's gaze was not malevolent, and her presence was fierce.

"The bad things keep happening to her," she says. "There is no place to escape."

Up came the sound bites of what trauma counselors call "intermittent reward-givers": caretakers who change on a dime, whose requirement of eggshell-treading will affect the nervous systems of those around them. *Why should I tell you the truth? I don't want to hear about how fucking hurt you are; this happens all the time in the literary world . . . How could you be so fucking stupid? . . .Would you still have a job if you'd made mistakes for two months on the job? Know what I think? I think you're just telling yourself you're forgetful, but you're not.You can't stay here if you keep making these mistakes . . .Who's it going to be in this family, you or me?*

Professional counselors mapped my history with the ruptures of loss and pain, calling them "traumatic events." I was mappable. These women had sex for money, had no home anymore, experienced rape in a daily basis. This kind of trauma did not figure in any form that could be traced, identified, quantified. The worst events possible seared their subjective spaces, severed their heads from their bodies so they could survive the aftermath of actual severance of heads from actual bodies.

"There is no way I could begin to truly understand the pain you have suffered," I said. "But I am a woman in the world who has felt pain. I have taken off my clothes for money. I have had an STI. I have been pregnant without meaning to be, without a husband and without money, and have not known what to do. I have lived in that cave of the bad things repeating themselves in my head. No one can imagine your pain. No one can pluck you out of the cave immediately. But this was a flashlight for me to start to climb out of my own cave, and I want you to have the flashlight. Just in case it helps." I breathed in and out, once. They looked at me.

"Even when someone is scary, when I am in that dark room, I can still do the simple exercise in the moment: I think of that fish with no water, and then, I imagine myself as the well, bringing water to the fish. I can close my eyes and do it very quickly, and sometimes, when I am in that room, it helps."

It sounded weak, I thought. Some women were with me; others were not, and they raised their hands. One woman with a bright green Congolese dress snapped her answer to Monica before stalking out of the room.

"She is saying what she has been through is so bad, and you have not been through it, and . . ." I could see that Monica felt a little bad translating this.

"It's a fair point," I told her.

Another hand went up, the heart-shaped face. Odette. Her voice was deep and strong, her words angry.

think people in your situation have anything like that."

I smiled at her, she was being kind, and so were the people who clapped. I also smiled a little to myself at the fact that I didn't have a badge for the UN compound. Being a perpetually broke twentysomething volunteer had its perks; no professional constraints kept me from offering personal stories that might build the bridge of words to these ladies. No practical considerations of my reputation or employability, either, keep me now from choosing to relate these details in writing—to not omit my own name. When I found out two-and-a-half *million* American high school girls have HPV and the number just went up from there, a commitment to every girl who has spent time in the room of sexual shame and pain overwhelmed a desire to keep private what might help the thirteen-year-old girl who hears that she has something, something dirtying her body, something shameful attached to her like a rumor or third nipple is attached. I was twenty-one, at a liberal university, the product of alternative education, a graduate of the Female Sexuality Workshop that started at Berkeley, and I still felt wretched. It has to be terribly lonely for that thirteen-year-old. And it must, I realized, be a wider circle than that one that includes the other STIs high schoolers encounter. No, wider. American college women too. Much wider: every infected body, every displaced person, every person with a discernible identity and every person without one, who has spent time in the room of sexual shame and pain. These women in their semicircle of plastic chairs must be even more lonely than that; the dissociative stress response that often grips rape victims or anyone who has been physically overpowered, removing her from presence in the moment, from her body, is not something victims can control. I choose to describe my experience as a sacred one for the women in that room simply because it's the only experience I have. I choose to see myself as pure, day after day cleansed with that well water. For her, sobbing, with braces and no driver's license; for her, sitting with her scarf wrapped about her head on a plastic chair with words like "Life Skills" blaring in all-caps on the wall.

"I imagined being the well healing myself for a long, long time before the terrible thoughts started to be less," I said. When Monica translated, she looked especially at Odette.

Odette's eyes were stormy yet clear at the same time. There was a fierceness to her challenge that gave me hope. She would not truly be lost, to us or to herself, her life would not be lost to her, unless and until she did not even believe in the words to communicate hopelessness. Only then, I thought, does hopelessness truly descend: when we cannot or will not even say the words to anyone: "I don't believe this will ever end." "I can't go on like this." She was fighting with me: she could still fight.

This is what I wrote to Odette when her pages-long email popped up on my ipod Touch, when the gadget by chance piggybacked on some public wireless in another traffic jam, this time in downtown nighttime Nairobi. I was in a taxi, on my way to a fancy hotel dinner with a poet. She was writing through a translator. *Thank you for being vulnerable and saying what happened to you, she wrote. I am very sorry. I want to believe what you said about thinking good thoughts to replace the bad ones but I soak in my own tears most of the time. I think about dying. I don't want to live like this anymore, to do this for money, but I don't know what else.*

I messaged Paul at GTZ about Odette's email. "She has identified you as a person to trust," he said. "Let us go to her home."

Introductory Creative Writing Exercise Series for Trauma Victims

Trauma victims are often unable to focus and feel calm and safe in their bodies due to unusual levels of stress hormones in their bodies, making access to their prefrontal cortex, which governs things like writing, nearly impossible. This exercise series is to help remedy that.

Exercise 1: Breath

Square breathing: Inhale through your nose for four long counts, hold it in for four long counts, and make a small "O" with your lips as though you're using a straw, then exhale for four long counts through your pursed lips. Hold for four counts before refilling your lungs with breath. Repeat four times. You may either keep your eyes open and softly focused on something in front of you during this exercise, or you may close them.

Exercise 2: Body

Emotional Freedom Technique, or "Tapping": Spend one inhale and one exhale lightly tapping each of the following places on your body.

The "third eye" space in the middle of the forehead.

The temples.

The cheekbones.

The "mustache area" above the upper lip.

The chin.

The fingertips, which you can do by tapping the fingers of both hands together.

The outside edge of each palm, from the wrist to the tip of the pinky and back. You can do this for both hands at once by lightly "karate chopping" along the edges of both hands together.

Exercise 3: Words

Repeat the tapping series, but this time students call out the answers to the following questions, which the teacher asks:

1. What's your name?
2. What's my name?

3. Where are we?
4. What's the weather like outside?
5. What's the year?
6. What's the month?
7. What day of the week is it?
8. What color are you wearing?

Exercise 4: Community

Highlights and Lowlights: The class sits in a circle or square, and goes round-robin style around the room, starting with the teacher, telling the following:

1. Name
2. Highlight: Something fun that happened today, or that they are grateful for.
3. Lowlight: Something annoying that happened today.

Students are allowed to "pass," and not say more than their name; and to choose two Highlights or Lowlights, or only choose a Highlight or a Lowlight. Allow some time for this exercise, especially if the group has been meeting for a while, as students often "save" stories to tell the group.

Exercise 5: Poem Creation

Metaphor

1. Everyone gets out a notebook and a writing implement. Make a collaborative list on the board of feelings students had during their Highlight and Lowlight stories. If someone's Highlight was a great sandwich for lunch, for example, both "hunger" and "satisfaction"

might be listed. If their Lowlight was a sleepless night, “tired” might be on the list, etc.

2. As a group, come up with metaphors that might be used to describe those feelings. Anger might be a fire in the belly, studying for an exam might be pushing a stone up the hill, etc. Happiness might be a warm wind through the trees. Again encourage specificity, and ask the students to write down the feeling and metaphor lists along with you as you write on the board.

3. Writing Time! “Take 10–15 minutes of quiet to write a poem (or a short-short story) beginning with a metaphor for one feeling and ending with another. You can use feelings from the list and metaphors generated there, or choose new ones of your own. You can choose a movement from happy to sad, or from peaceful to angry. Be sure to use specific imagery to create that progression from one feeling to another.”

4. Students may share if they’d like when the 15 minutes are up.

Exercise 6: Closure

Gratitude Circle: Round-robin around the room one more time, and everyone mentions something from class or someone else’s poem, or just from life in general, that they’re grateful for.

Purpose of This Exercise Series

The breathing exercise stimulates the parasympathetic nervous system, helping to reduce stress hormone levels and a state of autonomic arousal they create in trauma victims.

This allows the tapping exercise, which works with pressure points, to help “light up” the midline of the brain that governs body and spatial awareness. It will help create the possibility of holding a pen and the physical act of writing, which can be quite daunting for traumatized people.

The answering of questions while tapping can generate laughter and ease, and train the attention of a trauma victim to their surroundings. Both of these things aid with attention and focus, which traumatized people often lose without meaning to. (In that vein, it's advisable for the instructor to single out for admonishment any one student for "spacing out" or other forms of inattention.)

Highlights and Lowlights builds community faster than any other exercise I have used as an instructor. I have used it in different countries and languages, with groups of varying levels of skill and trauma experience. It is the bedrock of the empathy and engaged listening required for a safe space within which to write and share that writing. It helps substantially even when the workshop is merely one day.

Listing emotions helps students with identifying them, which is key to trauma recovery. Metaphors can further help provide them with a language to express them, and with ways to address them. That's why the progression piece of the poem assignment is important; key to trauma recovery is remembering that *feelings can change.*

Works Cited

Dillard, Annie. *The Writing Life.* New York: Harper & Row, 1989, 78–79.

Neruda, Pablo. "I Explain a Few Things." In Pablo Neruda, *Selected Poems: A Bilingual Edition*. Boston: Houghton Mifflin/Seymour Lawrence, 1970.

WHAT REMEMBERS US: RECITATION AND RECONSTITUTION IN *WINDFALL ROOM*

Zach Savich

What's more private than memorizing a poem? Not for performance, not for others, but to carry with you, to compose your mind. I used to do it all the time. There was a month in 2016 devoted to the first line of W. S. Merwin's "The Morning." I said it on the commuter train: "Would I love it this way if it could last." I muttered on the elevator: "Would I love it this way if it could last." The word "refrain" comes from the Latin *re* (of intensive force) and *frenum,* which is a bridle, or bit. The poem, repeated, sticks in your mouth. "Frenum" also gives us "frenulum," the fold of skin below the tongue, which supports and restrains. The refrain, in the mouth, bolsters the tongue.

One morning ("Would I love it this way if it could last"), I realized that I'd been hearing it wrong. I'd understood "this way" as a manner of loving: "Would I love it this way [that I love it now] if it could last." And I'd thought, "Of course I would. We don't love what we love because it will end; we love it because it's here." But if "it" is the morning, it can't last. The morning is made of change: light coming up, drying dew. Passing things. If you froze the scene, you'd lose it; thus, "this way" refers to the way in which the morning is here, which is momentary. The preserved eternal birdsong is no birdsong. The only way the morning "lasts" is by coming back. As it does. But we only do for so long. The line, I realized, is about our own brief ability to come back, for all our days. The fact of things not lasting isn't why we love them; if we're lucky, the fact of *our* not lasting is the only obstacle to love.

* * *

After that month of muttering, I memorized the rest of the poem in an hour, in the woods near the Wissahickon Creek in Philadelphia, a handwritten page on the overgrown trail. It ends:

> would I love it this way if I knew
> that I would remember anything that is
> here now anything anything

I hear the final "anything" as a request, into darkness. The thing that is "here now," in the end, is a desire for anything. ("Please one more / kiss in the kitchen / Before we turn the lights off," Merwin wrote after his wife's death.)

A private experience, this memorizing? And a communion.

* * *

The record skips ("anything anything"), the jukebox whirs, and I remember another poem I memorized, one afternoon in 2003. Its conclusion is also about memory and dissolution: Stanley Kunitz's "Touch Me" ("Touch me, / remind me who I am"). I'd driven three hours to go out in a traditional canoe. My friends never came. I sat on the dock and talked to myself, or Kunitz did: "Summer is late, my heart . . ."

There I am, at twenty, repeating an old man's love poem until its song of memory and forgetting becomes my memory, becomes a pattern that might hold me beyond forgetting. I made a small pile of stones for my friends, *dove sta memoria*, and put the page under it.

* * *

"The story of poetry has many beginnings," writes Jane Hirshfield in *Nine Gates*. "One is in Mnemosyne—Remembrance—earliest-born of the Greek goddesses, mother of the Muses and so also of the poem." But the memory stick of a poem doesn't make memory permanent or continuous. Rather, it buffers and refreshes, so that "the knowable world continues from moment to moment." The point isn't the memory but the continuing. The experience of a poem, like Merwin's morning, is made of passing impressions. It happens as it goes.

What lasts is echo, which comes back as plea ("anything anything") or a terminal invocation of the Muse ("remind me"). Of course, Remembrance is only the mother; the Muses don't bring memory but something further. The memorized poem doesn't just preserve. It companions, it prepares. What could be less private?

* * *

A calendar comes from it; the poems are mnemonic portals. A Sarah Gridley poem in that apartment without heat (2005). Carl Phillips' "Custom" in line at the post office (2006). A passage from Rosmarie Waldrop with hay fever and oysters, New Zealand (2007). Stanzas from Nathaniel Mackey in Maryland (2008). Pieces of Inger Christensen's *Alphabet*, driving through South Dakota (2009). Dickinson in Amherst, Hopkins in Houston.

The anthology is mine, is mind. If I started memorizing to help me write, to learn about poems from the inside, I continued because there are poems I want to have with me—as they are, not to take from, but to be with. I imagine a time when I can't read, when words fail, life falters, and I need them. Let them become me. "Remind me who I am." Isn't that what community offers?

* * *

And yet, as with any mantra-work, any playing of scales, the focus also opens you. First, there's the poem. Then, there's your life, which it comes to refer to, in ways you couldn't expect. I knew that Gridley poem, for example, "Prodigal Song," from *Weather Eye Open* (California, 2005). It says, "now you can imagine in what hour you are tempted, how far pleases / you best has shifted." I used it to calibrate: today, was I feeling more "how far pleases" (distant desires, desire for distance) or "how pleases me best has shifted" (located desire, acute, anew)?

While your mind is occupied with the words, the world can come in, in its minute and unsoundable rhythms.

* * *

Is it lonely if I say I felt this as community? It doesn't feel lonely, and it hasn't been. After an adolescent stint in chest-thumping performance scenes, I fell in with a crew of college poets. We were inspired or insufferable, probably both, but we were living by poetry. We'd recite at parties, talk in a collage of quotes, purl some Keats in unison, grow reverent as someone squinted at the ceiling where their memory of a sonnet lived. I danced with someone and she told me some Berrigan. I watched my friend mouthing to himself at a bus stop. Is prayer private? What if you share it?

Intensely private. And? Shared privacy. Which becomes intimacy, transmission, investment, tuning, our lives.

* * *

But I fell out of the habit. I even came to advocate, at times, for the benefits of forgetting, the sort that Lewis Hyde discusses in *A Primer for Forgetting*. He explores "the proposition that forgetfulness can be as useful as memory or, at the very least, that memory functions best in tandem with forgetting." He points out that Mnemosyne "is not simply Memory, for even as she helps humankind to remember the golden age" she also helps people, as Hesiod writes, "forget their heaviness and remember their sorrows not at all."

My stopping memorizing was partly getting older, partly years of cancer and its treatment, which fucked my memory, partly my interest, after living by poetry for more than a decade, to read in areas I had neglected. (I had assumed you could learn everything you needed to know about history and philosophy from poetry, which is true, but there's also reading widely as a poet.) And then I heard from Nick Maione: poet, painter, editor of the online journal *Windfall Room*.

* * *

Windfall Room, started in 2018, features films of poets reciting original work from memory. They're shot in a single-take, straight-on style, ideally in a setting that's meaningful to the poet and visually interesting. Featured poets include Alexis Almeida, Jericho Brown, Phil Metres, Zoe Tuck, many others. Why not more elaborate or artsy video-poems? "A marvelous thing happens as we watch a person give a great recitation," Maione explained in an interview for *Tupelo Quarterly*. "Their own face becomes even more a threshold of meaning, and their personality becomes infused and in communion with the universe of the poem; the person and the poem are there physically transfiguring and revealing each other, as well as the space they are in. A person with a poem inside them is enough."

The effect is private ("It brings the poet into a new relationship of presence with their own work," he says), but we share its record. Maione is especially interested in recitations by poets who don't typically memorize their work, who might not write poems with memorization in mind. What happens in the adaptation, the rendering of a poem into a performance for others, which highlights a private experience? It's different from what happens when a poem is adapted for, say, a reading in a bookstore or bar. In the past, I had sometimes memorized my poems while I was working on them and then forgotten them, favoring the next poem. And I had sometimes had one or two I could say from memory at readings, or if called to an unexpected stage, but I had mostly memorized others' work. (I already had too many of my own thoughts.) But Maione's invitation intrigued me. I started sitting with one of my recent poems, "Instructions," while riding a stationary bike, months into the pandemic, repeating to myself:

> Begin with a simple grammatical rule:
> Say the hardest thing you can, then look around.
> You don't have to write the hardest thing down.
> Say what you see when you turn . . .

I filmed my recitation with the basement's wood room glowing behind me. I don't know if my face became a "threshold of meaning"; tell me if you think so. Shortly after, I invited pieces for *Windfall Room* from a handful of poets who, like me, live in Northeast Ohio, and I helped organize other place-focused sets.

* * *

Sylvia Jones' "Turning the Head of a Rake on Its Side" is part of the Baltimore series edited by Dora Malech. It was filmed, Jones writes, "Lakeside at Druid Hill Park." Jones is seated on a low stone wall against a rusty fence, two looming apartment buildings behind her, past the weedy shores of the sunlit lake. It's as though one has come across her in repose on the path.

Her poem is one of visionary encounter with literary forebears, an antic pageant with echoes of the AWP (Association of Writers & Writing Programs) of Dante's afterworld. She starts, "Robitussin & tourmaline. I licked Gwendolyn Brooks' grave in a fever dream." That lick furthers the trip, but first there are phrases that evoke meditative, receptive divestment: "I was better with words when I wasn't with them," "little is new," "barely visible in the dust," "so much is different but I am not better." The residue of the fever dream then assembles into "literary dreams." "Carl Phillips plays me—playing myself," she says, suggesting how influence can become embodiment, a body swap that brings you back to yourself. "Norman Mailer gives me a handjob," she says. A hint of a laugh propels the next phrase. The poem ends in the bathroom of a party, with Susan Sontag and Philip Levine "together in perfect unison reciting Auden."

A recitation that ends with writers reciting, as though they are reciting not just a poem but "Auden" himself, pronouncing a name to summon another canonical presence. It isn't exactly comfortable, to my hearing, the literary dead's restless burlesque, with Phillips refracted through the narrator as guide. "A heavy desire to merge fabulism with reverence is what bore this piece," Jones wrote in a contributor's note. "More specifically, a quote from the Terrance Hayes poem 'Snow for Wallace Stevens': 'I too, having lost faith / in language, have placed my faith in language.'"

Sun in the scrappy grasses, fence shadows, velveteen lake—fabulism recounted among the everyday, a community of icons and ghosts, the poet alone on a wall, a faith in language, the perfect unison of the everyday.

* * *

Jones' recitation leaves me with a startled sense of the ordinary. The delivery, straight-forward, even deadpan, anchors the madcap scene, emphasizing, for me, the soberer moments ("So much is different but I am not better"). The location does, too: one on a walk might overhear someone speaking, from deep vision, and then continue on, succored and unsettled. In BJ Soloy's recitation of an excerpt from *HIM*, part of the Kansas City series edited by Jordan Stempleman, the effect is more of intimate address, of rumination and ritual that serves both particularity and mystery.

"This is from a prolonged elegy for Bill," Soloy writes. "It was filmed in front of a deconstructed piano at my sister-in-law's house in Iowa. It's ½ mile from where I was married, 1 mile from where I found out my dad died." He begins, offhand and aching: "A summer death is preferable to a winter's death, for the pliable surface of the idiot earth," and I hear the depth of place, the sense of affected air opening outward, in phrases that follow: "sheetless sleep and windows open—can you tell."

Soloy's wavy, greying hair is to his shoulders. At about 30 seconds in ("a winter's death is preferable"), a figure in a white, ruffled shirt appears, stands behind Soloy, and tenderly gathers his hair. This, he told me later, is his wife, Julie, playing the role of "the ceremonial butcher." She smooths some strands of the brow back and reaches behind her for some scissors. She cuts in steady snips—you can hear the resistance, the many gathered strands—and at about one minute in ("Oklahoma City is a city of white pick-ups in the rain"), she hands the locks to the poet, who has been reciting all this time, as though in a parallel plane, body and voice, and departs. He holds the hair to his chest. He touches it with his other hand. He holds it before him. After the last lines ("Everyone looks like you today, old man, even those that don't look like you, even the parked cars, even the people"), he tosses the tufts gently in the air.

* * *

A recitation, perhaps, is a similar scattering: a released dove, bouquet to the wind, cut strings of fate, the issue of the body, which was the self, becoming otherwise. In Jason Harris' "Deforestation," part of the series of Northeast Ohio poets that I edited, the self that's changed is both individual and environmental. "'Deforestation' is a poem written about Sandy Ridge Reservation, a small marshland 22 miles outside of Cleveland, Ohio," Harris writes. "The marshland is surrounded by home developments. The day this poem came to life, I was bird-watching. Through my binoculars, I could see—between the small opening of trees—construction workers taking down trees near a slew of newly built homes."

It begins with the poet in freefall: "Fast, that's how I fell, headfirst, from the slender bill of a blackbird." (As with the poems above, I'm representing the lines as I heard them, without the lineation or punctuation that appears in printed versions.) He's thrown into a lush scene, "a marsh filled with egrets, sandhill cranes, cirrus clouds empty-bodied and fragrant." That final phrase is marvelous: it puts us in the clouds, which are empty, yet, being "empty-bodied," they are also "bodied." Then there's a stunning moment, as Harris recites, rain on his glasses, with the grey of Lake Erie behind him blurring into the grey of the clouds, the horizon a disintegrating, eiderdown partition. "It," he says, "the Black boy—wait—I meant bird." At "wait," he looks to the side, smiles. Has he erred in the recitation? Or is the error, and its correction, that deliberate slippage, which at once foregrounds and transforms Blackness in his pastoral, part of the poem? "There I was, minding no one's business but my own," he concludes, again gesturing to a self asserted and subsumed, "falling"—and here the wind picks up, as though summoned—"headfirst, and fast."

* * *

I asked Harris about that Black boy / blackbird moment. Was it in the poem, as written, or in the recitation? "The Black boy/bird line is in the poem," he replied. "Interestingly, when I was at the marsh and writing the poem, I intended to write blackbird but did actually write Black boy. The accident in the creation of the poem eventually found its way back into the poem." In memorizing, we return to the live iteration of the "accident in the creation." We think it through anew. It becomes us.

* * *

Community isn't just about shared places and perspectives; it's about how meaning is generated and what those meanings activate and invite, for us, individually, as we move through our wider lives. These recitations *tune* me, through the intimacy of their exchange and their record of intensely personal experience, just as my experiences memorizing poems brought me closer to the language of others. Maione has said, "I hope it highlights that a poem is made by a person and that a person has a body and especially a face and therefore all the capacity and the art and grace to have their own presence be part of the experience of the work if they wish it to be." Community, in this conception, radiates out from the presences we know and live by heart.

Exercises

1. The *Windfall Room* Standard: Memorize a poem you've written. Maybe one that you didn't write with performance in mind. Film yourself reciting it in a meaningful location.

2. Constructivist *Windfall Room* Standard: Go to a meaningful location. Compose a poem, only in memory. Don't write it down. Come back to the location for as long as you want, repeat. Film yourself reciting it.

3. Inspired by Sylvia Jones: In Jones' poem, an imagined ritual of homage ("I licked Gwendolyn Brooks' grave in a fever dream") leads to visionary encounters with literary forebears. Make a list of writers who you'd like to hear your work. Who's in the audience? Choose one and imagine a ritual that creates a connection via a physical item and the body. "I floated on Etel Adnan's paintings in a flood." "I put a lock of Milton's hair next to my ear." Journey forward from there, incorporating other writers from your list.

4. Inspired by BJ Soloy: Soloy writes, of the poem he recited, "I juggled many poems and chose this one because of an elision (between recitation, ceremony, memory, and elegy) that seems amplified when spoken to an audience beyond the page. It's a poem from a short collection of elegiac stuff for my dad and the domestic/public space always negotiated in art seems particularly dynamic when the domestic space and its intimacy have been abandoned in death by one party. With the supposed apostrophic audience forfeiting the game, the public becomes all that's left, aside from the speaking self, who gets plenty of airtime anyway." Write a poem that focuses on a loss, or absence. Address it to a general public that may be "all that's left." Imagine that they might vanish as soon as you stop speaking.

5. Inspired by Jason Harris: Go somewhere in nature. Write a poem from the perspective of one "falling headfirst, fast" toward the setting. Maintain a slow pace.

6. For Only Yours: Memorize a poem, by you or someone else, that you will ever only recite to one person. Do so.

Works Cited

"A New Relationship of Presence: An Interview with Nick Maione, conducted by Zach Savich," www.tupeloquarterly.com/editors-feature/a-new-relationship-of-presence-an-interview-with-nick-maione-conducted-by-zach-savich/.

Hayes, Terrance. "Snow for Wallace Stevens." In *Lighthead*. New York: Penguin Group, 2010.

Hirshfield, Jane. *Nine Gates*. New York: Harper Perennial, 1998.

Jones, Sylvia. "Turning the Head of a Rake on Its Side," https://poetrysocietyny.org/spiltmilk/2020/8/10/two-poems-by-sylvia-jones.

Kunitz, Stanley. "Touch Me." In *Passing Through*. New York: W. W. Norton, 1995.

Merwin, W. S. "The Morning." In *Garden Time*. Port Townsend, WA: Copper Canyon, 2016.

CONTRIBUTORS

Traci Brimhall is a university distinguished professor of creative writing and narrative medicine at Kansas State University. She is the author of five collections of poetry, most recently *Love Prodigal* (Copper Canyon, 2024). Known for her poems that often marry the ordinary with the surreal, Brimhall's work has appeared widely in journals and magazines such as the *New Yorker*, *Orion*, the *New Republic*, *Poetry*, the *Nation*, and the *New York Times Magazine*. Through fellowships with the National Endowment of the Arts, National Parks Service, and Academy of American Poets she's taught writing workshops in farm schools, art museums, libraries, medical communities, and the outdoors. She's also received a Karnes Fellowships through Purdue Library's Special Collections to study the lost poem drafts of Amelia Earhart. She is the current poet laureate of Kansas.

Chris Campanioni's work on migration and media theory has been awarded the Calder Prize for interdisciplinary research and a Mellon Foundation fellowship, and his writing has received the Pushcart Prize, International Latino Book Award, and Academy of American Poets College Prize. His essays, poetry, and fiction have been translated into Spanish and Portuguese and have found a home in several venues, including *Best American Essays* and *Latin American Literature Today*. Recent books include a novel named *VHS* (CLASH Books, 2025), a creative nonfiction called *north by north/west* (West Virginia University Press, 2025), a notebook titled *A and B and Also Nothing* (Unbound Edition, 2023), and the poetry collection *Windows 85* (Roof Books, 2024). He teaches creative writing and media studies as the writer in residence at Pace University in New York City.

Wendy Chen is the author of the novel *Their Divine Fires* (Algonquin Books, 2024) and the poetry collection *Unearthings* (Tavern Books, 2018). Her poetry translations of Song-dynasty woman writer Li Qingzhao are published in a collection titled *The Magpie at Night* (Farrar, Straus & Giroux, 2025). She is the editor of *Figure 1*, associate editor-in-chief of *Tupelo Quarterly*, and prose editor of Tupelo Press. Her poetry, translations, and prose have appeared in *Freeman's*, *A Public Space*, *Lit* Hub, and elsewhere. She earned her MFA in poetry from Syracuse University and her PhD in English from the University of Denver. Currently, she is an assistant professor of creative writing at the University of Nevada, Las Vegas.

Kristina Marie Darling is the author of over thirty books, which include recent releases from Bloomsbury, Dzanc, Persea, and Penguin Canada. A twice-awarded Fulbright Scholar, Dr. Darling's work has also been recognized with multiple endowed residences at Yaddo, a 2024 Villa Lena Foundation Fellowship, eleven juried residencies at the American Academy in Rome, and a nomination for the Distinguished Visitor Fellowship at the American Academy in Berlin. A prolific educator and public speaker, she has held academic appointments at the American University of Rome, the Universidade do Porto, the European Law and Governance School, the Amsterdam School for Cultural Analysis, the American Research Center in Sofia, the Leysin American School in Switzerland, and the Ionion Center for the Arts and Culture in Greece, where she serves as permanent faculty. Dr. Darling has also spearheaded a number of recent philanthropic projects in Europe, establishing a scholarship fund for first-generation college students to have their first experience abroad as part of an international writing community, as well as a grant program for former humanitarian aid workers to come to Kefalonia and tell their stories. In addition to these philanthropic projects, she has served on fellowship juries for Yaddo, Fulbright, Millay, the

2010), won the 2010 T. S. Eliot Poetry Prize. His 2014 collection *Landscape Portrait Figure Form* (Omnidawn, 2014) was named by the *Barnes & Noble Review* as a Best Poetry Book. Other titles include his poetry collection *Self-Portrait as Wikipedia Entry* (Copper Canyon, 2017) and the anthologies *Native Voices: Contemporary Indigenous Poetry, Craft, and Conversations* (Tupelo, 2019) and *Bullets into Bells: Poets and Citizens Respond to Gun Violence* (Beacon, 2017). Rader writes and reviews regularly for the *San Francisco Chronicle*, the *Huffington Post*, *BOMB*, *Ploughshares*, *Artforum*, and the *Los Angeles Review of Books*, where he co-authors a poetry column with Victoria Chang. In 2020, he was a finalist for the National Book Critics Circle Balakian Award. His most recent book, *Before the Borderless: Dialogues with the Art of Cy Twombly* (Copper Canyon, 2023), was named by *Bookriot* as one of ten "mesmerizing" books of modern poetry. Rader's writing has been supported by fellowships from Princeton University, Harvard University, the MacDowell Foundation, Art Omi, and the Headlands Center for the Arts. He is a 2019 Guggenheim Fellow in poetry and a professor at the University of San Francisco.

Zach Savich's latest book is the hybrid critical-memoir-for-performance *A Field of Telephones* (53rd State, 2025). He is also the author of seven collections of poetry, including *Momently* (Black Ocean, 2024), and several chapbooks, limited-edition volumes, and books of prose. His work has received the Iowa Poetry Prize, the Colorado Prize for Poetry, the CSU Poetry Center's Open Book Award, and other honors, including residencies from the Vermont Studio Center, ArtPark, and the Chautauqua Institution. His writing has appeared in journals and anthologies including *American Poetry Review*, *Best New Poets*, *Boston Review*, *Georgia Review*, and *Poetry Northwest*. Savich teaches at the Cleveland Institute of Art and serves as co-editor of Rescue Press's Open Prose Series.

"She says she cannot stop having the bad thoughts because what happened with her is so terrible," translated Monica. "She just can't stop having the terrible thoughts."

There's a physiological process behind what Odette described and a name for it: limbic hijack. Trauma victims undergo what's called "spinning out" or "fretting," that hideous subjective spiral of all things helpless and hopeless. To add insult to the injury of terrible feeling, it blocks focus and access to learned systems: letters, numbers, reading, where you left your keys. It's why perfectly smart people forget, in the moment, how to dial 911.

Some of the women, a couple of the older ones, smiled up at me, and others had disengaged. To spend more than a moment in an appropriately alarming situation in limbic hijack is hell on earth. These women continued to spend years there. Even if their situation improved and they knew consciously that things were fine, their system would for a long while continue to release hormones arguing otherwise—and it's impossible to reverse the activity of our brain stem, or "lizard brain," in the short term. The brain stem is the source of fight-or-flight chemicals and impulsive actions (there is a reason it's called "bulimia *nervosa*," for example) but not the other, more "refined" reactions. Those come from the part of the brain that stores a great deal of our personality: our memories, our wisdom—the part of the brain that pretty much shuts down during limbic hijack. We can't access our wisdom, our memories, ourselves. It is an interiority governed by bleakness, by the certainty that nothing is all right or will ever be, that one has lost oneself. Refugees have already lost their exterior home; for the duration of their trauma and a good while after, they lose their interior one too. In this respect, "Internally Displaced Person" could have more than one meaning.

Monica finished translating my words about the flashlight to the sex workers and turned to me. A smattering of applause as I sat down. She whispered, "Thank you for being vulnerable to them. They don't

Kimmel Harding Nelson Center for the Arts, the Helene Wurlitzer Foundation, and many other awards in the United States and abroad. Born and raised in the American Midwest, she now divides her time between Greece, Spain, and the Amalfi Coast.

Ming Lauren Holden is the author of *Refuge* (2018), which was chosen by Lidia Yuknavitch as the winner of the inaugural Kore Press Memoir Award. Holden's next book, *Fire Alarm*, is forthcoming from Tupelo Press. Holden's fiction won the *Glimmer Train* Family Matters Fiction Prize; her poetry won the *Bellingham Review*'s 49th Parallel Award for Poetry; and her nonfiction won the *Chattahoochee Review*'s Lamar York Nonfiction Prize. She has worked in over twenty countries since 2001, most often in the humanitarian sector focusing on refugee advocacy. She earned her BA from Brown University, her MFA from Indiana University, and her PhD from the University of California, Santa Barbara. She works as a freelance consultant, teacher, editor, and artist on the Mediterranean coast.

John James is the author of *The Milk Hours* (Milkweed, 2019), selected by Henri Cole for the Max Ritvo Poetry Prize, as well as three chapbooks, most recently *Extinction Song* (Tupelo, 2026), winner of the Snowbound Chapbook Award. Recent poems appear in *New England Review*, the *Hopkins Review*, *Ninth Letter*, *Best American Poetry*, the Academy of American Poets' *Poem-a-Day*, and elsewhere. His work has been supported by fellowships and awards from the Bread Loaf Environmental Writers Conference, the Academy of American Poets, and the Lannan Center for Poetics and Social Practice at Georgetown University. He holds an MFA in creative writing from Columbia and is completing a PhD in English at the University of California, Berkeley.

Dean Rader has authored or co-authored twelve books. His debut collection of poems, *Works & Days* (Truman State University Press,

2010), won the 2010 T. S. Eliot Poetry Prize. His 2014 collection *Landscape Portrait Figure Form* (Omnidawn, 2014) was named by the *Barnes & Noble Review* as a Best Poetry Book. Other titles include his poetry collection *Self-Portrait as Wikipedia Entry* (Copper Canyon, 2017) and the anthologies *Native Voices: Contemporary Indigenous Poetry, Craft, and Conversations* (Tupelo, 2019) and *Bullets into Bells: Poets and Citizens Respond to Gun Violence* (Beacon, 2017). Rader writes and reviews regularly for the *San Francisco Chronicle*, the *Huffington Post*, *BOMB*, *Ploughshares*, *Artforum*, and the *Los Angeles Review of Books*, where he co-authors a poetry column with Victoria Chang. In 2020, he was a finalist for the National Book Critics Circle Balakian Award. His most recent book, *Before the Borderless: Dialogues with the Art of Cy Twombly* (Copper Canyon, 2023), was named by *Bookriot* as one of ten "mesmerizing" books of modern poetry. Rader's writing has been supported by fellowships from Princeton University, Harvard University, the MacDowell Foundation, Art Omi, and the Headlands Center for the Arts. He is a 2019 Guggenheim Fellow in poetry and a professor at the University of San Francisco.

Zach Savich's latest book is the hybrid critical-memoir-for-performance *A Field of Telephones* (53rd State, 2025). He is also the author of seven collections of poetry, including *Momently* (Black Ocean, 2024), and several chapbooks, limited-edition volumes, and books of prose. His work has received the Iowa Poetry Prize, the Colorado Prize for Poetry, the CSU Poetry Center's Open Book Award, and other honors, including residencies from the Vermont Studio Center, ArtPark, and the Chautauqua Institution. His writing has appeared in journals and anthologies including *American Poetry Review*, *Best New Poets*, *Boston Review*, *Georgia Review*, and *Poetry Northwest*. Savich teaches at the Cleveland Institute of Art and serves as co-editor of Rescue Press's Open Prose Series.